Powerfully Recovered!

Powerfully Recovered!

A Confirmed 12 Stepper Challenges the Movement

Anne Wayman

Universal Publishers/UPUBLISH.COM
http://upublish.com

Universal Publishers/UPUBLISH.COM, ISBN: 1-58112-876-2
www.upublish.com/books/wayman.htm

NOTE: Five percent of the author's net income from the sale
of paper copies of this book will be used to replace the trees
used in its production and to develop sustainable sources of
paper.

Powerfully Recovered web site:
http://www.powerfullyrecovered.com

As always, to my daughter Linda, and my two sons, Michael (and Mike's wife, Gloria) and Stephen – each has been more supportive than they know.

To my grandchildren, Emily Rose and her brother Ben. They've taught me love at a whole new level.

To the readers of the First Edition, and to the many who sent me supportive notes.

And, of course, to the God/Goddess/Source of my understanding – such as it is.

Contents

Introduction

My name is Anne Wayman. I've been sober and clean in Alcoholics Anonymous (A.A.) and Narcotics Anonymous (N.A.) over 25 years. I have participated in Al-Anon, Debtors Anonymous (D.A.), Co-Dependents Anonymous (CODA), Adult Children of Alcoholics (ACoA) and have even gone to a few Artists Anonymous (Art-Anon) meetings.

Today, I have no interest in drinking alcohol or using drugs. This has been so for many years. This doesn't mean I'm 'cured' or invulnerable to a slip, for neither is true. But the Program has given me the promised freedom from practicing my addiction to alcohol and other drugs.

Adding Al-Anon, CODA, and ACoA to my basic A.A. and N.A. taught me not only that I can't control others, but gave me the inner resources I need, so control – of myself or others – is rarely an issue. As a result my relationships with friends, lovers and business associates are much better.

Time in D.A. means I now handle my money well. My brief attendance at Artists Anonymous meetings showed me how the Steps apply to my professional life and helped me realize I'm not the only writer who gets stuck or has trouble explaining my wacko work schedule to non-writers.

In other words, the practice of the 12 Steps has worked well for me as it has for literally millions of others.

Like most, the changes in my life happened slowly. During my first year of sobriety, for instance, I attended over 400 meetings and followed most of my sponsor's suggestions. I came close to drinking and using a number of times, worked the Steps, and generally hung on.

Gradually, after several years, I was able to reduce my meetings to two or three a week, which meant I could spend more time with my children. I was also able to do 12 Step work, and act in various 12 Step service capacities. My work became less erratic. I fell in and out of love without falling completely apart. My life, and my response to it, became more balanced.

A Sense Of Constriction

For years, A.A. and the other 12 Step groups were my way of life. But there came a time when I began to feel constricted in the Fellowship. The way of life I had struggled to adopt and which had, without question, saved my life, started to feel stifling and limiting.

Unsure of what was happening to me, I went to more meetings, and then to different meetings. I got more involved with service. I led a meeting in a mental hospital and volunteered to make coffee as often as I could. I took on more speaking opportunities and wrote more inventories and sponsored more people, all to no avail. My restlessness and discontent grew.

Slowly it dawned on me that this restlessness did not include a desire to drink alcohol, use drugs or practice my other dysfunctions. Gradually I dropped my 12 Step commitments and began to gently explore the world beyond the recovery Fellowship.

To my surprise I found that less involvement in recovery and more involvement in the world left me feeling more serene. New experiences meant new opportunities to grow, and the 12 Steps worked outside the Fellowship as well as they did inside.

Something else important happened too. By allowing my world to enlarge, I was able to view myself from a different perspective. In time I came to know that I am much more than an alcoholic/drug addict with a co-dependency problem.

Today I know that I am not powerless; I know that I am not sick. In fact, I am powerfully recovered, just as the 12 Steps promise.

Claim Of Power

To find and claim my empowerment, to become willing to accept that I am recovered, I had first to look beyond recovery, and then return to a deeper understanding of the 12 Steps. For to claim that I am powerfully recovered might appear to fly in the face of conventional 12 Step thought.

Typically, 12 Steppers convince themselves and each other that they are perpetually powerless and that their recovery is never-ending. These ideas, in spite of their popularity, are not part of the 12 Step Program.

Instead, they are myths that have grown up over time – myths that stem from fear and a misunderstanding of the original 12 Step literature.

The 12 Step Program, as it was originally conceived, is a program of empowerment, aimed at becoming recovered. Unfortunately, few understand this today, and as a result 12 Steppers are prevented from reaching their full potential.

Failure In The Ghetto

As if that weren't bad enough, the myths of never-ending recovery and perpetual powerlessness make a significant contribution to the relative failure of the 12 Step movement to make a real impact on some who need it most – those in the inner cities and ghettos.

Telling people who have little, if any, experience with success, that they can never successfully recover guarantees that many of them will never even try. Insisting that people who already feel powerless must adopt an attitude of perpetual powerlessness in order to let go of their addiction means many of them will refuse to even attempt to work the Program.

Critics

There has recently been serious criticism of the 12 Step movement. Much of this comes from people outside the movement who see 12 Steppers as stuck in one way or another. While some of these complaints are ill founded, much is valid.

I believe that all these problems stem from 12 Steppers' insistence on hanging on to the myths of never-ending recovery and perpetual powerlessness.

My own experiences, and those shared with me by many others, both inside and outside the 12 Step movement, have compelled me to write this book. I am convinced we must examine, and let go of, the myths that damage us individually and hurt the movement as a whole.

Had A.A.'s founders stuck with the then established beliefs about alcoholism, they would have died drunk. It was their willingness to look beyond conventional wisdom that resulted in their success and the success of the millions of us that have followed in their footsteps.

A Challenge

In the book, *Alcoholics Anonymous*,[1] the original source of the whole 12 Step movement, the statement is made, in Chapter 11:

We realize we know only a little. (p. 164)

This humble statement encourages us to explore, to learn, and to expand – just as A.A.'s founders did.

---

[1] All quotations from the *Big Book* come from the third edition printed in paperback in 1966.

The second Appendix of *Alcoholics Anonymous*, titled
Spiritual Experience, closes with the following quote from
Herbert Spencer:

> There is a principle which is a bar against
> all information, which is proof against all
> arguments and which cannot fail to keep a
> person in everlasting ignorance – that is
> the principle of contempt prior to
> investigation. (A.A. p. 570)

It is in this spirit that I challenge you to examine the
myths of recovery.

Consider how believing in never-ending recovery and
perpetual powerlessness limits you and others. Dare to
imagine how accepting full recovery and true empowerment
might be. Allow your mind to soar as you picture how this
would affect not only you, but others.

As 12 Steppers we know the value of self-examination
and have experienced the letting go of old ideas that prevent
us from growing. We know how to separate fear and wishful
thinking from courage and acceptance.

The myths of never-ending recovery and perpetual
powerlessness are old ideas. We can turn and face them, and
let them go – knowing we stand on firm ground.

We can move beyond the myths and continue on the
road to full freedom, with the Program as our foundation
.   We have the power to choose.

Author's Notes

All sorts of things come up during the writing of a book. These notes will give you an idea about some of my thinking – particularly in areas where I'm not following the accepted wisdom.

An Anonymity Break

Yes, Anne Wayman is my real name. Yes, I am breaking anonymity.

The primary reason is because I'm questioning the customary thinking found in 12 Step groups and I can't justify hiding who I am when making such a challenge. I believe you have a right to know who is speaking out.

You'll find more of my thinking on anonymity in Appendix 1 of this book.

Sexist Language And 12 Step Literature

The books, *Alcoholics Anonymous* and *The Twelve Steps and Twelve Traditions*, are the original source material for all 12 Step Programs. They were written in 1939 and 1955 respectively, and made use of what was then considered correct generics "he," "him," etc. when referring to people and to God. As yet there has been no updating of the sexist language in subsequent editions, although there has been some talk about creating special editions that would eliminate what are now recognized as sexist references.

Because I believe the way we use language reflects and influences our deepest beliefs, I have taken the liberty of changing these generic, masculine references to gender neutral references in all quotes. I've used *The Handbook of Nonsexist Writing* by Casey Miller and Kate Swift, published by Barnes and Noble Books, 1980, as a definitive guide.

About The First Edition

As a published writer, I first created a book proposal and submitted it through my agent. I received 19 positive rejections from major and minor publishing houses. That is, each sent a personal letter complimenting me on my grasp of the subject matter, my writing and the concept in general. However each of these letters also said "not for us."

I determined to self-publish. This posed another problem – I lacked the cash! I put some of the text on the World Wide Web and sold a few home-printed copies to people who stumbled on to the site.

The project languished on the Web for a couple of years. I moved; I changed jobs more than once.

Always preferring to freelance, I became the San Diego Guide for About (http://sandiego.about.com), a content and portal site working to help people through the morass of information on the Web. Among the 700+ Guides to a variety of subjects is the Writer's Exchange (http://writerexchange.about.com) where I found a link to Upublish: http://www.upublish.com

Upublish is a leader in on-demand publishing. Here I could get my book published, for a reasonable price because it's printed only when someone buys it.

About The Second Edition

This edition is a direct result of my experience with the first. Print-on-demand (POD) has proven to be a viable publishing method for many. Potential readers are willing to order from the net. Book distributions have opened up to include POD books so brick and mortar bookstores can offer them. Ebooks have also enjoyed great success.

More importantly for me, readers like the book!

Reader acceptance has encouraged me to update the book and make it more acceptable for bookstores. That means the four-color cover, a redesign of the text presentation, and an expansion of the resources and the addition of the cartoons.

Marketing through the net has meant international connections. The cartoons were drawn in Australia by Narcosis who has a site at: http://fly.to/dragoncomix. Kara and Ian created the cover in Canada: http://www.time4somethingelse.com. However, the English is American and I've drawn on America for research.

I've tried to become less provincial with this edition by expanding my own awareness and including some international resources.

The original eight chapters are the same – with some minor updating and correction.

Comments are appreciated. I can be reached via email at: wayman@inetworld.net Web pages for this book are at: http://www.powerfullyrecovered.com

You'll find additional contact information in the back of the book.

Chapter 1

12 Step Truth – 12 Step Myth

Is (freedom from our addiction/dysfunction) all that we can expect ...No, (it) is only the first gift ...a new life of endless possibilities can be lived if we are willing ...(p. 8)[2]

---

[2] The quotes at the beginning of each chapter come from *As Bill Sees It*.

Today, people entering a 12 Step program quickly adopt a series of ideas that, if summed up, would sound something like this:

> I am a (name the condition). (Name the condition) is an incurable disease which means my recovery is never-ending. Because my recovery is never-ending, I am perpetually powerless.

Of course, no one ever puts it exactly this way. Instead, 12 Steppers talk a great deal about their past and current problems and successes with letting go of their addictive/dysfunctional behavior. If you listen closely, however, you'll find the emphasis is only on partial recovery. That is, they talk and act as if their recovery is endless instead of discussing how they might fulfill the potential of the Program.

Nonetheless, even with this limited view, there have been impressive results. Literally millions of alcoholics around the world have quit drinking through the original 12 Step group, Alcoholics Anonymous. More millions have stopped using other drugs, learned to handle food in a healthy way, mastered money, stopped compulsive gambling, and found new and productive ways to relate to themselves and others through one or more of the alphabet soup of 12 Step organizations.

Something Is Wrong

Even with all these accomplishments, however, something is wrong with the 12 Step movement. Although 12 Step Programs have helped millions, they haven't come close to reaching their full promise – there are many more millions who could be helped.

Members Get Stuck

Instead of using the 12 Step Programs to heal and get on with living life, 12 Steppers tend to get stuck in their program(s).

The most obvious example of this is the way so many members limit their friendships and experiences to those found within the confines of 12 Step culture. More than a few brag that their whole lives are built around meetings and the people they meet there.

Often this bragging is accompanied with disparaging remarks about those not involved in 12 Step work. 'Normies,' as these people are often called, are seen as incapable of understanding the recovering person and therefore difficult or impossible to get along with.

The symptoms of being stuck in this way can be more subtle. Some refuse to consider dating non-12 Steppers; others insist on going to meetings at the expense of their families even after such a sacrifice is no longer needed. Still others use the fact of their addiction/dysfunction as an excuse for taking responsibilities at work or at home.

The Program that is supposed to help people get back into the world they rejected through their addiction/dysfunction has, for many instead, become another reason to feel separate and isolated from the greater whole of life.

An Important Distinction

On my sponsor's recommendation, I started my Fourth Step right around 60 days. I went around in a fog of confusion and fear for the better part of a week.

I thought I'd found salvation when, at the grocery store, I ran into a woman I knew from meetings. Marge had several years of sobriety, making her an expert in my eyes at the time.

She asked how I was doing and I stammered something about getting ready to start my inventory.

"You haven't been sober long enough," she exclaimed, obviously horrified.

I rushed home and called my sponsor. "Marge says it's too soon to do my inventory," I cried.

"Anne," he sighed, "you'll hear anything you want to hear from people in and around A.A. and you don't know the Program well enough to know if they are giving you good advice or not."

He went on to refer me to Dr. Bob's story – you know, where he does all six steps (there were only six then, but they encompassed everything our 12 do) in a long evening.

He then talked a bit about the difference between the Fellowship and the Program, pointing out that the fellowship is our experience, strength, hope and personal opinion. "The Program," he said, "is the *Big Book* and the *Twelve and Twelve*. Even conference approved literature falls more in the Fellowship category than pure Program."

Later we talked about it some more and he gave me some advice I've found to be good and true.

"If someone tells you to do or not to do something and you don't know if it squares with the Program," he said, "ask them to show you where it says that in the Big Book or the Twelve and Twelve.

"One of two things will happen. Either they will show you and you'll have to come to terms with it if you want to stay sober, or, if it's only their opinion, they will leave you alone."

Many Never Try

Then there is the large number of people who want recovery, but refuse the 12 Step approach. Of course, for some, the refusal to participate in a 12 Step Program is simply another form of denial and/or resistance. However, many others refuse to participate in a system that seems to insist they remain locked into never-ending recovery and perpetual powerlessness.

This is most notably true in the inner cities and ghettos. Insisting on never-ending recovery and perpetual powerlessness is particularly unattractive there. This phenomenon is discussed thoroughly in Chapter 7.

Old-Timers Leave

There aren't many old-timers at meetings. Although just how long a person has to be successful in a 12 Step program to become an old-timer is debatable, the fact that we don't see many isn't. And it isn't because they've slipped.

The myths of perpetual powerlessness and never-ending recovery have become so entrenched that those who grow beyond them find themselves subject to much subtle criticism and even overt rebuke.

When this happens, many move on. As a result, much wisdom is lost – the very wisdom that could solve the problems we're talking about.

There's no denying it. In spite of real success, the 12 Step movement has failed to reach its full potential.

The Myths Of Recovery

The cause of this failure is not the 12 Step Programs themselves. The Steps are clear.

Rather, the problems come from two deceptive myths that have developed within 12 Step Fellowships over the years since the Program was first developed.

These myths tell us that:

- recovery is never-ending, and,
- addiction/dysfunction makes people perpetually powerless.

Although each of these ideas may appear to help people in the early stages of recovery, they are actually untrue. Ultimately, they prevent many 12 Step members from moving fully into life, as well as keeping many others from ever joining in the first place.

It's important to note that neither idea was present in the beginning of what has grown to be known as the 12 Step movement. Quite the contrary, in fact. These limiting myths have developed over time as the 12 Step movement has grown.

Both ideas come, for the most part, from the cautionary stories told at meetings. They are told over and over again, and rarely, if ever, challenged. As a result, members adopt these notions as part of their belief systems. They are passed on with a certainty that is rarely questioned. As a result, some stories have taken on the power of myth.

Of course, all myths must begin somewhere, and understanding their origin helps us analyze their full impact. The roots of the myth of never-ending recovery can be found as the disease theory of addiction gained credence. This is discussed in Chapter 2. The myth of perpetual powerlessness, however, has its beginnings in the very founding of the program itself, as discussed in Chapter 3.

Part of the reason the myths are perpetuated is continuing confusion over the difference between the Fellowship and the Program.

The Fellowship v. The Program

Alcoholics Anonymous began with a meeting. The story is well known. Bill W. was totally unable to control or eliminate his drinking until he was introduced to the Oxford Movement rules or guidelines. On a business trip he was sorely tempted to drink, but instead arranged to talk with a practicing drunk. That alcoholic was Dr. Bob, another Oxford member, who, as a result, of their conversations, was also able to quit drinking. Dr. Bob's last drink was on June 10, 1935, which is also considered the A.A.'s founding. Together, they co-founded A.A. largely by talking with other alcoholics.

Before long, the (men)[3] began to meet regularly to discuss their recovery. The number of meetings increased as more people got sober, and the nascent organization referred to those participating as the "Fellowship."

But there is a huge, and important, difference between the 12 Step Program and the 12 Step Fellowship.

The Fellowship is made up of the people who participate in a 12 Step group or meeting.[4] All who show up are considered members, whether they are free from their addiction/dysfunction or not and whether they practice the 12 Steps or not. As individual members of the Fellowship, we share our stories – what has come to be known as our "experience, strength, and hope" with each other in a variety of situations, including meetings. Much of this sharing is about our own experience with the 12 Step Program, but much of it is not.

---

[3] The early members of Alcoholics Anonymous were almost exclusively men. See Chapter 3.

[4] This includes regularly scheduled meetings, online meetings, informal meetings over coffee, the correspondence of Loners – anywhere and any way 12 Steppers get together to discuss their recovery.

It is exactly the "sharing of our own experience" that makes the distinction between the Program and the Fellowship important.

The Distinction Is Important

As important and vital, as the sharing of stories is to the recovery process, those stories are also a major source of the damaging myths of perpetual powerlessness and never-ending recovery.

It's easy to see why – when we remember that our stories are filtered through our own experience and opinion. When we forget this, and even when we don't, those opinions may get passed along as fact, taking on much more importance than they actually deserve.

This is not to negate the value of our stories, or even our opinions, not at all. But it is important to remember that not everything we hear at meetings or over coffee accurately reflects the 12 Step Program.

The Program

The Program grew out of the early Fellowship. By 1939 about 100 people had gotten sober as a result of Dr. Bob's and Bill W.'s efforts. With the help of others, Bill W. wrote the book, *Alcoholics Anonymous.* It is here that the 12 Step Program, as we have it today, was formalized, including the 12 Steps.

The first 164 pages of the Big Book have remained unchanged, except for minor copy editing, in subsequent editions.

These 164 pages are the original source material for *all* 12 Step Programs.

By the late 1940s and early 50s, because of A.A.'s growth, it became evident that more explanation about the Steps was needed. It also became obvious that some sort of organizational structure for the groups was necessary. After much discussion, the organizational principles, known as the Twelve Traditions, were written.

The Traditions and their explanation were combined with an explanation for each of the 12 Steps in a book called the *Twelve Steps and Twelve Traditions*, published by A.A. World Services, Inc. in 1952. Known as the *12 and 12*, it too was largely written by Bill W. It is considered the textbook for the Steps and Traditions and is also original source material for the 12 Step movement as a whole.

Thus, the 12 Step Program itself is contained in the first 164 pages of the *Big Book* and in the chapters dealing with the Steps in the *12 and 12*. What is written there is the Program – no more, no less. Only the name of the addiction/dysfunction need be changed to apply the Program to other conditions.

Some of the newer 12 Step organizations have published their own books on the addiction/dysfunction they address. Each draws on *the Big Book* and the *12 and 12* and in one way or another, acknowledges these sources as the bedrock foundation of the 12 Step Program.

This is not to say that other books, as well as audio tapes, movies and videos about 12 Step Recovery are without value. Obviously many have contributed a great deal, both to individual recovery and to the growth of the movement as a whole. But those, like this book, fall under the rubric of the Fellowship rather than the Program, and should be viewed as such.[5]

---

[5] Some feel that any *conference approved literature* – that is literature put out by the official organization of a 12 Step group like A.A., N.A., etc. – is also Program. I disagree. Obviously, I use some of that literature – as in the quotes here from *As Bill Sees It* – but it isn't part of the original source material, and therefore, in my opinion, not part of Program It's not unusual to find some watering down of the Program in later publications, no matter who approves them.

The Promises

One of the unwritten laws of the 12 Step movement is, "if it ain't broke, don't fix it." Many would argue that the benefits of the 12 Step movement are so great that there's no point in worrying about the myths of never-ending recovery and perpetual powerlessness.

It is true that many millions have found real relief from their addiction/dysfunction through one 12 Step Program or another. In that sense, the movement is working.

However, to insist that our recovery is never-ending and that we must remain perpetually powerless to stay free from our addiction /dysfunction is to remain locked in fear. Less fear, to be sure, than we experienced practicing our addiction/dysfunction, but real fear nonetheless. And fear is the opposite of what we're actually promised. Giving up the myths is the antidote to the fear. Letting go of the myths opens the path to more freedom and growth.

The implications of giving up these myths of recovery, however, are much larger than the empowerment of any individual member.

Asserting we are never recovered and perpetually powerless is anything but attractive. These beliefs mean that many who would otherwise be helped are not.

In short, the movement is not working as well as it could be. The whole goal of the 12 Steps is recovery in the fullest sense of the word. This fact is most obviously evidenced in what has become known as "The Promises."

The Promises are, for the most part, contained in a single paragraph in the sixth chapter of the *Big Book*, where it is made clear they will come true as a result of working the 12 Steps. Just as freedom from addiction/dysfunction is the primary purpose of the Program, so The Promises are its overall goal. They pledge, if we work the Program, we will:

> ...know a new freedom and a new
> happiness. We will not regret the past nor

> wish to shut the door on it. We will
> comprehend the word serenity and know
> peace ...we will see how our experience
> benefits others. That feeling of uselessness
> and self-pity will disappear... Our whole
> attitude and outlook upon life will change.
> Fear of people and economic insecurity will
> leave us. . . We will intuitively know how
> to handle situations which used to baffle
> us. (A.A., pp. 82-83)

Obviously, these promises are the antithesis of fear and powerlessness. We are promised the ability to handle our lives with grace and elegance, to choose, to act, to do – informed by our experience.

We can become powerfully recovered. To deny this fact is to deceive and limit ourselves, and others. We have only to be willing to work for it.

Chapter 2

The Myth Of Never-Ending Recovery

We must never be blinded by the futile philosophy that we are just hapless victims . . . We have to believe that we can really choose. (p. 4)

Twelve Step groups deliver two, decidedly mixed messages. On one hand, we are assured that if we work the Program, we need never again be victimized by our addiction/dysfunction. On the other hand, we are told over and over again that our recovery will be never-ending.

The first is true, but severely limited by the second. For 12 Steppers, the word 'recovery' has gotten linked with the disease theory of addiction. As a result, the myth that recovery is never-ending leads us to believe we are always sick.

This is best shown in the saying heard at many meetings, *I'm just a sick (name the condition)*. Instead of enjoying the Promises of the Program, this saying indicates how stuck we can become.

The Disease Theory Of Addiction

The possibility that addiction might be a disease was considered as early as the late 1700s. But the more prevalent view in the United States, until the 1930s and 1940s, was that alcoholism and other drug addictions were moral issues. The Temperance Movement's solution was to exhort people to use willpower and sign oaths never to use 'demon' alcohol again. People who pledged and failed were seen as lacking moral fiber and 'backbone.'

When A.A. was formed in the early 1930s, members quickly realized that drunks were more open to the idea they could quit drinking if alcoholism was presented as an 'illness,' 'physical malady' or even an 'allergy' rather than as a moral issue. So we find references to alcoholism as a disease in the *Big Book* and in other early references. A.A. also had the support of some doctors who added credence to the disease theory.

In those early days, however, alcoholism as a disease was emphasized only as a way to reduce prejudice. Not only was it easier to get someone to accept help for a disease, it was also easier to get their employer, banker, and even their family to give them another chance. But, once someone was on the road to recovery, the disease theory didn't matter much one way or the other.

Over-Emphasis Of The Disease Theory

As A.A. grew and word of its success spread, interest in, and acceptance of addiction as a disease grew gradually. It wasn't until Dr. E. M. Jellinek of Johns Hopkins University published *The Disease Theory of Alcoholism* in 1960 that the over-emphasis on the disease theory really began to take hold. Blow-ups of his diagram of the course of alcoholism began to appear in A.A. meeting rooms. It charted the alcoholic from the appearance of normal drinking down to circles of death or insanity unless treatment intervened.

As his paper and chart made its way into the popular press, insurance companies began funding residence recovery programs. A new focus on addiction-as-disease developed.

Slowly, the idea that addiction is a disease seeped into our consciousness. Everyone from treatment centers to radio talk shows began to refer to addicts as 'sick' people. Women's and men's magazines had articles attempting to explain the disease.

Not surprisingly, the idea that we are 'sick' people began to show up in the stories we told at meetings. The emphasis from disease as a way to open doors had switched to disease as a way of being.

It was during this period too, that 12 Step groups addressing problems other than alcoholism began to grow. Since A.A. members originally formed most of these groups, it's not surprising that everything from co-dependency to debt was labeled an addictive disease.

How We Think And Feel About Disease

The word, disease, has decidedly negative connotations. Illnesses like colds and flu make us feel terrible. Others, like heart disease and AIDS, cause impairment and shorten life if not properly treated. Still others, Alzheimer's and the Ebola virus, are almost always fatal. Being sick is the opposite of the healthy, good feelings we all want.

Another way to say this is that when a person is sick, they don't function well, and feel anything but powerful.

The over-emphasis of the disease theory of addiction leads addicts, at least unconsciously, to think of themselves as sick long after they have ceased using their drug/destructive behavior of choice.

"I am" Is A Powerful Statement

It is well documented that repeating an idea about ourselves over and over again has an effect. Positive ideas tend to strengthen our view of ourselves; negative ones strengthen our negative view. Adding "I am" to such ideas makes them even more potent.

The "I am a (name the condition)" statement we make in 12 Step meetings is an example of how effective these affirmations can be. We all recognize the benefits.

When a newcomer is willing to introduce themselves this way, it is a strong indication that they have at least begun to accept the nature of their condition. At a minimum, they have made the first half of the First Step.[6]

Most of us remember clearly how fearful we were the first time we used that phrase, "I am (name the condition)" and how relieved we were to have finally said it out loud. It was indeed a major part of our initial healing. As our recovery continues, the "I am" statement serves not only to keep us in touch with the nature of our addiction, but is helpful to newcomers as well, assuring them they are not alone.

But, look at what also happens as we repeat over and over again, "I am (name the condition.)" Because we have learned to think of addiction as a disease from which we can never become recovered, we are also saying, in effect, "I am sick." Over time, this rather negative attitude permeates our entire view of ourselves.

We Are Much More Than Our Condition

The real problem with over-identifying with the disease aspects of our addiction/dysfunction is that it limits our view of ourselves. With that perspective, we tend to see everything in our lives through the lens of addiction. As long as we believe we can never become recovered, we operate from a base of fear.

Although we may be addicted, the truth is each one of us is much more than our addiction/dysfunction. We are parents or children, male or female. We each have special talents. We succeed at some things and don't do so well with others.

When we look at the whole of our lives, after we've gotten some solid recovery time, we find that our addiction is really a small part of who we are. Certainly it's an important part – the experience it gives us often allows us to help

---

[6] The First Step is: "We admitted we were powerless over (name the condition) –that our lives had become unmanageable."

others, as well as acting as a 'reminder' not to use our substance/behavior of choice. But it isn't, and shouldn't be, the whole of how we see ourselves – that's just too limiting. The way I like to say this for myself is:

> Yes, I am a recovered alcoholic. That fact is as important and as unimportant as the fact that I am female.

Sometimes my gender is important, sometimes it's not. But, like my addiction, it will always be there.

What might happen if, when we felt ready, we said instead:

> I am a recovered (name the condition)?

Recovered!

I'd been sober about nine months when I went to a discussion meeting I'd never attended before. We were in the middle of the preliminaries when a fellow I'd never seen walked in. He looked rough, with his shoulder length graying hair, a leather vest and biker boots. He sat next to me with a wink of his blue eyes and I could see his hands were scarred and lumpy;

The leader then asked us to introduce ourselves and say how much sobriety we had. I was startled when the fellow next to me said, slowly and clearly, "My name is Ray. I'm a recovered alcoholic and I've been clean and sober 19 years."

You could feel the shock in the room in the moment of frozen silence before introductions continued. Most of us had less than a year, a couple had two or three years, and one had 11.

The leader asked for a discussion topic and a member with three years spoke up about how she would always be in recovery, and that she believed that anyone saying they were recovered was in danger of a slip – no matter how much time they had. Talk continued with those speaking agreeing. Finally, Ray spoke up.

> "My name is Ray," he repeated, "and I'm a recovered alcoholic."
>
> He went on to tell a bit of his drunk-a-log and more about his recovery. He talked about a time when he'd come close to a slip and gotten back into the Big Book.
>
> "I was reading the Foreword to the First Edition and it dawned on me they said they were 'recovered.' I read it several times, and the rest of the book over a few days. I kept coming back to that Foreword. Read it yourselves and decide."
>
> I went home in a horrible state of confusion and read the Foreword as he suggested. It did indeed talk about how the Pioneers were recovered, which flew in the face of everything I'd heard around the tables. The next day I told my sponsor what had happened. Much to my surprise, he grinned.
>
> "That must have been Ray," he said, and then went on. "Don't worry about it now; with luck and work, there will come a time when it will make more sense to you."

We Can Be Recover_ed_

Although few realize it, the first 164 pages of *The Big Book* use the term 'recovered' at least 11 times.[7] The first two sentences of Foreword to the First Edition use 'recovered' twice:

> We, of Alcoholics Anonymous, are more than one hundred men and women who have recovered from a seemingly hopeless state of mind and body. To show other alcoholics *precisely how we have recovered*

---

[7] Pages xiii, xxiii, 17, 20, 29, 45, 90, 96, 113, 132, and 133. I started counting several times before I discovered the closest thing to a concordance to *The Big Book – A Reference Guide to the Big Book of Alcoholics Anonymous* by Stewert C., published by Recovery Press, 1986.

is the main purpose of this book. (Emphasis
theirs; A.A. p. xiii)

Chapter 2, "There Is a Solution," uses 'recovered' three
times. It's interesting to note how clearly that chapter makes
'recovered' a real possibility. It doesn't matter if the authors
are talking about other members or themselves. Here are the
three phrases:

> Nearly all have recovered. They have
> solved the drink problem. (A.A. p. 17)

> ...you are curious to discover how and why
> ...we have recovered ..." (A.A., p. 20)

> ...showing how we recovered. (A.A., p. 29)

There really is no question about it –

> Obviously "...showing how we recovered"
> is the purpose and goal of *The Big Book's*
> second chapter.

On the other hand, 'recovering' is used only twice, once
in Chapter 8, "To Wives" and again in Chapter 9, "The
Family Afterward." In both cases, the thrust is advice about
how families can help their newcomer family member,
particularly in the beginning. But even in these chapters,
'recovered' is used three times.

Obviously, becoming recover*ed* was, and still is the
goal. Not only is it the goal, but, according to the *Big Book*,
becoming recovered is possible, even likely.

What's The Problem?

Why, then, do 12 Steppers insist they are forever recovering,
never recovered? There are many reasons in addition to
over-identification with addiction-as-disease, including:

• confusion about what "normal" really means,

- misunderstanding about what "recovered" really means,
- unnecessary fear of relapse,
- confusion about humility, and,
- fear of becoming recovered.

Clearing up these confusions and fears goes a long way toward making sense of what recovery and recovered really mean.

Addiction Is Not A Normal State

One of the things often said by 12 Steppers is: I'm a (*name the condition*); my normal state is to practice that addiction. This simply is not true!

While the nature of addiction is to keep practicing the addiction, it is hardly normal. The behavior that results from the addiction cannot be called normal under any circumstances – as well we know.

In fact, the idea that it is normal to practice an addiction may hide denial. There's something plaintive and victim-like in such a notion. It's as if there's an undercurrent of wishing we could return to our substance/dysfunction but in moderation.

But that's not what the Program is all about. The whole purpose of the Program is to help us get back to normal, to balance ...to be "restored to sanity." (A.A. p. 84)

Failure To Recognize Abstaining Is Normal

One of the strangest things we do is talk as if abstaining from a substance and/or behavior is somehow abnormal. While we were practicing it seemed as if our addiction/dysfunction was normal, but the truth is, it wasn't. In spite of our perceptions, most people don't abuse alcohol or drugs; nor do they practice the destructive behaviors that 12 Step groups address.

When we come to the Program, we tend to separate ourselves from those who are not in our 12 Step Program. We do this at first because it simply makes sense to avoid hanging out with the people we practiced our addiction with.

But this practical approach gets twisted when we begin to separate ourselves from all people who are not in a 12 Step Program, even those who are not addicted. People in the Fellowship often refer to the non-addicted as 'normies.' Unfortunately, using the term 'normies' comes to mean we are somehow special. We claim that either they don't understand us or we don't understand them. Although there are some important differences, they mostly center on addiction and recovery – beyond that we're more alike than different.

Since we use the term 'normie' when we are clean and sober, we begin to think of ourselves as abnormal or not-normal – even though we are no longer practicing our addiction!

If we think this through, we can see how strange our thinking has become. Abstaining is a major part of what being restored to sanity is all about, and much closer to 'normal' than not.

Confusion About What 'Recovered' Really Means

We're also confused about what 'recovered' really means. When someone says they are recovered, someone else is sure to tell them they are in danger of a slip. This is often followed up with a story about how someone started thinking they had their addiction licked only to find themselves back practicing it again.

In the parlance of the Fellowship, 'recovered' has become confused with 'cure'.

'Recovered' doesn't mean we can return to our addiction/dysfunction in some 'normal' fashion. On the contrary, recovered means we are free from our addiction/dysfunction. To be free means not only do we no longer practice our addiction, but that we are released from any desire to do so.

The *Big Book* makes it clear; we can be recovered if we work all the Steps, and when we do, we needn't fear relapse.

Unnecessary Fear of Relapse

The fear of relapse, or a slip, is at least in the beginning of recovery, a real one. Hard statistics are impossible to gather from 12 Step groups because of their anonymous nature, but anyone attending a 12 Step group regularly quickly discovers that not everyone lets go of their addiction. People disappear from meetings, and some of them return to tell the story of how they thought they could control their addiction with the new knowledge they gained at the meetings only to discover things were worse than before. Often their struggles are horrendous.

These cautionary tales often strike fear into the hearts of newcomers, and remind those who have been successful for longer that they are not invulnerable. Word filters back that someone who went out on a slip will never come back because they died.

But, if we practice the program with willingness and honesty and thoroughness, we needn't fear relapse. The *Big Book* reassures us, shortly after the Promises, that, although we are never cured, we do not need to fear relapse. It says:

> For by this time sanity will have returned. We will seldom be interested in liquor. If tempted, we recoil from it as from a hot flame. We react sanely and normally, and we will find this has happened automatically. We will see that our new attitude toward liquor has been given to us without any thought or effort on our part. It just comes. We are not fighting it, neither are we avoiding the temptation. We feel as though we had been placed in a

position of neutrality–safe and protected.
We have not even sworn off. Instead, the
problem has been removed. It does not
exist for us. We are neither cocky nor are
we afraid. That is our experience. That is
how we react so long as we keep in fit
spiritual condition. (A.A. pp. 84-85)

This statement appears after some serious homework
which needs be done before these additional 12 Step
Promises come true – following Step 10.

Step 10 is the first of what have become known as the
Maintenance Steps. It is in the continuing maintenance or
practice of Steps 10, 11, and 12 that we find our power and
become truly recovered.

Chapter 3

The Myth Of Perpetual Powerlessness

*People are supposed to think, and act. They weren't made
. . .to be automatons.* (p. 55)

In meeting after meeting, 12 Steppers continually assure themselves and each other that they are powerless – not only over their addiction/dysfunction, but over everything else in their lives as well.

These statements are rarely questioned, which is rather odd if you think about it. Powerlessness is, after all, a rather nasty concept. It's defined as:

> **devoid of strength or resources; lacking authority or capacity to act.**

Why would a group of people who have taken major action to improve their lives insist that they are powerless? If you listen to 12 Steppers very long you might be tempted to believe that 12 Step Program demands their members shun any sort of power at all. This notion is far from the truth. The 12 Steps actually show the way to balanced, ethical personal empowerment.

The perpetual powerlessness many 12 Steppers espouse is simply myth – myth that not only prevents them from stepping fully into life, but limits their effectiveness with others who want to recover as well.

To understand the myth of perpetual powerlessness and the damage it does, we need first to look at what the word, 'power' actually means.

The Meaning Of Power

The origin of our word, 'power,' is the French word, 'poeir,' which means: *to be able.* Thus power is defined in part, as: *the ability to act or produce an effect.* In other words, each time we take action to do anything (or we decide to take no action at all) we are using our power.

It's the other parts of the definition that cause problems. Power is further defined as: *possession of control, authority . . .over others.* Because this kind of power is subject to so much abuse, 12 Steppers are inclined to assume that power of any sort is bad.

Of course, there is nothing inherent in either control or authority, even 'over others,' that is abusive. Instead, the offenses stem from underlying, and often, unconscious motives that drive the exploitation of that power.

We'll see, in Chapter 4 how the 12 Steps provide us with ways we can be trusted with power, but let's first examine the myth of perpetual powerlessness.

Society's View Of Power

Twelve-Step groups operate within a cultural context. In the United States our view of power is, at best, scrambled. The country was founded in a rebellion against misused power. Our democracy was designed to make sure citizens were not powerless. We have a representative form of government backed up with the Bill of Rights, which gives people a say in what happens.

But this country has also experienced tremendous misuse of power. In many ways it's been built on exploitation – of people, most notably in the case of slavery and the way we've treated the American Indian and other people of color – of property and of resources. Although most of the overt forms of exploitation are gone, their legacy lingers in both thought and action. Women still receive significantly less pay for equal work; people of color still experience prejudice, and the poor tend to be ghettoized or homeless. Political scandals continue to rock the nation. The ever-widening gap between people with lots of money and people with less money, creates additional unease, for in our society money tends to equal power. The abuse of the environment continues in spite of increased awareness about global warming and its consequences. In fact, the problems we face often seem overwhelming.

Given these facts, it's small wonder we have a mixed relationship with power – we've seen and even experienced its abuse; we've felt helpless in the face of power. On the other hand, many of us have, if we're honest, felt the rush that comes with having power.

Not surprisingly, this confusion about power is reflected in 12 Step groups as well, particularly about power as it affects individuals. But the muddle has specific foundations in the movement as well.

Within the 12 Step movement, the myth of perpetual powerlessness originates from three sources:

Pioneer Influence

Alcoholics Anonymous, the grandfather – and I use the gender-specific term consciously – of all the 12 Step Recovery Programs, was co-founded by a white, male stockbroker and a white male physician in the 1930s. The race, gender and occupation of these gentlemen are important because their attitudes, and the attitudes of their era, had a profound influence on the organization they created – an influence that continues today.

There have been no demographic studies on the first members and groups of A.A. It is, however, possible to glean valuable clues about the early membership from the "Personal Stories" section in the book, *Alcoholics Anonymous*. The stories there are personal histories of recovery, written anonymously, with an eye toward helping others identify their own alcoholism and begin to work the program.

Part 1 is called "Pioneers of A.A." There are 13 stories, including Dr. Bob's, one of A.A.'s co-founders. (Bill W's story is told in the first chapter of the *Big Book*.) All 13 got sober in the early years of A.A. and are considered a representative population of the organization in the early days.

Of the 14, including Bill W., three were women.[8]

Apparently all were white – Jim's Story, (A.A. p. 483), the history of the African-American physician who founded A.A.'s first Black[9] group, is told in another section which was first published in 1955. His race is emphasized there, making it clear he was an exception.

Only one of the pioneers grew up poor, and, according to her story, she married into money.

The rest were middle class (in an era where the middle class had relatively more spendable income than it does today), upper middle class and wealthy. In fact, it's startling to read these stories and recognize the emphasis that was put on money and education. It's safe to say the Pioneers were concerned with class.

These demographics in no way disparage the Pioneers' experiences. The stories of their drunkenness are universally shocking and heart rending; their contact with A.A. and subsequent recovery were truly miraculous. Each pioneer made a significant contribution to the establishment and growth of Alcoholics Anonymous.

---

[8] This works out to 21.4 percent and is undoubtedly high for the time. In fact, it's amazing they found 3 women willing to tell their stories. Even today, women make up only about 34 percent of the membership, while women make up 51 percent of the country's total population.

[9] The need for a separate, Black group is also reflective of the times, even as late as the mid '50s. Although there are special interest groups – that is women's groups, men's groups, gay and lesbian groups, etc., it is rare to find a group today based solely on race. (See also Chapter 8.)

However, understanding something about the background, and, if you will, class, of these Pioneers helps us understand something about the 12 Step movement today.

The Pioneers Were NOT Powerless

The truth is that most of the early A.A. members were successful, educated and, in most cases wealthy white men. Their major problem was alcoholism. Once they quit drinking, they had the resources to put their lives back together with minimum fuss.

In short, they were not powerless people – not before they began to drink to excess, nor after they had quit drinking. On the contrary, most of them had real power as it was then, and is currently defined in our society.

Because, on the whole, they had money and influence, they were in a position to be tempted to abuse their power – a temptation not limited to alcoholics by any means.

Bill W., by his own admission, had an obsession with being, as he put it, "A Number One man ..." [10] at whatever he tried. In the same version of his story he talks about his experience on Wall Street and remembers how, when he returned from fighting in World War I he was "spurred (by) the same old power drive." [11] He goes on to relate that he was "drinking to dream great dreams of greater power."[12] When he at last sobered up it isn't surprising that he felt he must let go of his drive to power if he were to stay sober. His personal beliefs were, naturally enough, reflected in his writings.

Since most of the other early A.A. members were also far from powerless, it's also not surprising that they didn't question this emphasis on the problems associated with power.

---

[10] *Alcoholics Anonymous Comes of Age*, p. 53
[11] Ibid., p. 54
[12] Ibid., p. 55

Not only that, but much of A.A.'s early history is strewn with stories of power gone awry. Many of the groups dreamed grand dreams of large and profitable recovery centers that would not only help drunks get sober, and would wield influence far and wide, but would make their founders wealthy as well.

All these ventures were doomed to failure, largely, it can be supposed, because the motivations were personal glory rather than service. Individuals trying to exercise control over others in their [13] Step groups also created problems.

As a result, power as the ability to act was overlooked, and abusive, controlling power was rightfully warned against. Since no distinction about the type of power was made, power in general became feared.

Of course, the face of 12 Step groups has changed as the movement has grown. Programs dealing with dysfunctional behaviors have led the way in showing how many people with addictive behavior lack self-worth and how increasing self-worth – personal empowerment – is vital for recovery. Plus, the sheer number of members means there is no real opportunity for any one person to take over anything for any length of time.

But the idea that power is to be shunned has continued. It shows up most often in the stories we continue to tell; stories which are often couched in how powerless we are – about anything and everything that goes on in our lives.

Part of this continued insistence on powerlessness comes from generalizing the First Step.

---

[13] Adapted from Step 3, *Made a decision to turn our will and our lives over to God as we understood Him.* By substituting "God" for "him," sexism is avoided.

Generalization Of The First Step

The First Step reads: We admitted we were powerless over (name the condition)–that our lives had become unmanageable.

It's interesting to note that this is the only place the word 'powerless' appears in the *Big Book*. No place else are we asked to admit powerlessness, and here we are asked only to admit powerlessness over our addiction/dysfunction.

Granted, it is the feeling of powerlessness or helplessness – *devoid of strength or resources; lacking the ...capacity to act* – over the addiction or dysfunction that drives most to Program in the first place. Without a sense of hopelessness, there would be little motivation to change. It is in the recognition and admission of powerlessness over the addiction/dysfunction that healing actually begins. The First Step is both our acceptance of our addiction/dysfunction, and the beginning of the change we desire so much.

This sense of powerlessness, however, was never intended to become a constant life theme. It is, instead, a beginning point, a place to start.

What is usually overlooked is that the acceptance of our powerlessness over the addiction/dysfunction is, in itself, a powerful act. Even though we were motivated by hopelessness and fear, we took action, powerful action.

It's easier to understand the First Step as a starting place when we recognize that it, like all the other Steps, is written in the past tense. Step 1 reads:

We admitted we *were* powerless ... not
We admit we *are* powerless ... (Emphasis mine.)

The difference is tremendously significant, yet I've never heard it discussed at any 12 Step meeting. Remember, the *Big Book* was written with the purpose of showing:

...alcoholics precisely how we recovered.
(Original emphasis, A.A. p. xiii)

Again, note the use of the past tense. The authors were claiming that in the past they were powerless over alcohol, but had found a way, had discovered a series of actions, had found the power, to quit practicing their addiction.

For an alcoholic, staying sober is hardly a powerless position. The same can be said of anyone who has been victimized by any addiction or dysfunction and recovered.

Of course, there is nothing in the Steps that advises us against using them in other areas of our lives. Quite the contrary, in fact. The 12 Step urges us to *practice these principles in all our affairs*, and there are times when we can apply the admission of powerlessness to other life-issues as well as to our addiction/dysfunction. But admitting I'm powerless over a particular life-issue is a far cry from claiming to be powerless over my whole life. Such a claim is actually a denial of the Promises.

Taking the First Step is a powerful action – each Step is a powerful action we take on our own behalf.

Powerful Action

I'd been sober almost two years. I arrived late at the speaker's meeting, which meant I got to stand at the back with other latecomers and those who weren't sure they needed to be there at all. I was pleased when Bob showed up; he had at least 15 years and I respected him.

A well-polished young man approached the podium, introduced himself as an alcoholic, told us he had six years and proceeded with his drunk-a-log.

Toward the end of his talk he began to tell us what his life was like now. Part of this story was about a new job he had just accepted. He told how bored he'd been in his previous job and how delighted he'd been when the new opportunity surfaced. He then talked about how he'd gone to his sponsor for "permission" to take the new job.

"Didn't he say he had six years on the Program," I whispered to Bob.

> "That's what I heard him say."
> "Did he really say he had to get permission from his sponsor before he accepted the new job . . .the one he really wanted?"
> "That's what I heard him say," Bob replied again, this time with a raised eyebrow as if to ask me what I thought of that proposition.
> "I quit a job a couple of months ago," I responded. "I talked it over with my sponsor... in fact I guess I really wanted him to make the decision for me, but he wouldn't. He said I needed to learn how to run my own life. At first I didn't know what to do. Finally I realized that the issue wasn't about sobriety − I wasn't going to get drunk over this no matter what decision I made. So I went ahead − it was scary, but it's turned out well."
> "Sounds like both of you used some wisdom," Bob said with a twinkle of approval in his eyes.

Surrender, Humility And Power

There is much talk of surrender and humility in 12 Step groups. The concepts are worth looking at for there is much misunderstanding of both ideas.

Of Surrender

"Surrender" is another of those words that isn't used in *The Big Book,* not even once as near as I can tell. You'll often hear it used in the Fellowship, however, when one urges another to "surrender to God."

If you ask how this relates to the Program, you'll probably be told it's a short form on the Third Step, but that isn't what the Step 3 says. It reads:

> Made a decision to turn our will and our lives over to the care of God as we understand God.[14]

There's powerful action in this step:

---

[14] Remember, I use gender-neutral terms.

- First, we're being asked to make a decision, to choose.
- Next, we're asked to "...turn our will and our lives over to the *care* of God." (Emphasis mine.)

A friend of mine puts it this way:

> It's like this. If I turn my car over to my mechanic I probably won't ever see it again; if I turn my car over to the care of my mechanic, I expect it to come back to me repaired.

It's a subtle, but important distinction. When we buy into the idea that God's going to take care of everything for us, we're giving up our power and escaping responsibility. On the other hand, when we ask that we be in the *care* of our Higher Power we're setting up a spiritual context for our lives. It's this context that allows us to act powerfully on our own behalf and to experience one of the most exciting promises:

> We will intuitively know how to handle situations which used to baffle us. (A.A. p. 84)

Appendix II, "Spiritual Experience," describes the results we can expect this way:

> With few exceptions our members find that they have tapped an unsuspected inner resource. . . (A.A. p. 569-570)

"Intuitively know how to handle..." and tapping into "...an unsuspected inner resource" are pretty good definitions of personal empowerment.

But What About Surrender?

The word, surrender, is often used to defend the myth of perpetual powerlessness because it conjures a picture of 'giving up' as when we wave a white flag. But let's look at some more definitions from Webster's New Collegiate Dictionary.

The root of the word, surrender, comes from the French word, *surrendre* which means to give back, yield. Yield has a wide variety of meanings, including:

> to give or render as fitting, rightfully owed ...to give up ...and even: to be fruitful or productive.

Note that each requires an action, and, as we said, power is the ability to act. With this in mind, claiming perpetual powerlessness in all aspects of our lives seems off the mark. Actually, claiming to be perpetually powerless may be an actual denial of God's will for us. Which, in my experience, brings us directly to the question of humility.

Real Humility

Humility is one of the Program's most misunderstood concepts. It gets all confused with humiliation, false pride and even self-worth. Let's again start with some definitions.

The Webster's New Collegiate tells us that the word, 'humble,' comes from the French word, 'humus,' which means 'earth.'

Humble is defined as *not . . .haughty: not arrogant..* Haughtiness and arrogance are surely to be avoided. They usually come out of feelings of inferiority and the attempt to make ourselves feel better by putting others down.

But this definition is framed in what 'humble' is not. We still don't know what it might be. It's tempting to look at the French root and state that being humble is closely related to being grounded, and although my intuition agrees, I've not been able to verify that through standard dictionaries. I offer it here as food for thought as you work through to your own definition.

However, the *12 and 12* addresses humility in the discussion of Step 7.[15] There it defines humility as:

...the desire to seek and do God's will.[16]

This is a powerful and effective definition. It requires honest self-searching, getting quiet (even grounded), learning to hear, and discovering how to trust the 'still small voice' of our 'inner resources.'

When humility is coupled with the admonition in the 10th Step to admit promptly when we are wrong, we've made major progress in finding and acting on God's will for us.

It's worth pointing out here as well, that the *12 and 12's* discussion of the 10th Step [17]includes the statement that inventories:

...are not always to be taken in red ink.[18]

This is aimed at the tendency 12 Steppers have toward self-abasement and even the misplaced pride at being worse than our peers in the Program. We are responsible to know what's good about ourselves, as well as what's bad and what's in between – in other words a balanced view.

This balanced view of ourselves is empowering in and of itself. When we know and accept our strengths as well as our weaknesses and all that's in between, we are able to act in positive ways, for ourselves and others.

---

[15] Step 7 reads: *Humbly asked God to remove our shortcomings.* (Yes, I've again changed the generic Him to the less generic-specific word, God.)

[16] *12 and 12*, p. 72

[17] Step 10 reads: *Continued to take personal inventory and when we were wrong, promptly admitted it.*

[18] *12 and 12*, p. 93

Self-Worth And Addiction/Dysfunction

There is general agreement that people coming to a 12 Step program are lacking in true self-worth or self-esteem. Instead, we often have a kind of false-pride that acts as a cover for our behavior. We live in fear that our true nature will be discovered. We are afraid that our innate goodness is permanently damaged, if it was ever there in the first place.

Often we seem to glory in our defects. We see this in the number of times we play a sort of "top you" in our stories – we want to demonstrate that we were at least as bad as others, or even worse than anyone else. Our views of ourselves are a long way from balanced and claiming perpetual powerlessness simply reinforces the lack of balance.

Self-worth is the opposite of the selfishness and self-centeredness we experienced while we were practicing our addiction/dysfunction. Self-worth allows us to act in a powerful (empowered) manner without the selfishness of the power drive.

What happens when you tell someone, particularly someone who is lacking in a balanced view of themselves, over and over again that they are powerless? They become or stay fearful, tentative and full of self-doubt. People who are told they are powerless come to believe it, and they act from that position – afraid to take risks. Or they act out in rebellion, stomping on others in an attempt to feel some strength.

As long as 12 Steppers continue to insist that they are perpetually powerless, the movement and its members will fail to reach their full potential.

The 12 Step Program is a Program requiring great individual and collective action – it is a Program of Power.

Chapter 4

Twelve Step Power

...a new life of endless possibilities can be lived if we are willing to continue our awakening ...(p. 10)

A lthough the myths of perpetual powerlessness and never-ending recovery obscure the fact, the 12 Steps spell out exactly how members can become powerfully recovered.

Even without the myths, however, the process to full healing can seem mysterious, even hidden, at first. A closer look, however, makes it clear.

The Mystery of 12 Step Power

Although it's rarely stated in just this way, the practice of the 12 Steps is a spiritual discipline. This becomes obvious when we look at the 12th Step, which promises:

> ...a spiritual awakening as a result of these steps ...

Of course, the exact nature of this spiritual awakening is left to individual discovery. While some have a single spiritual experience as Bill W. did, by far the majority experience a continuing and increasing spiritual awareness and effectiveness. This is often known as the 'educational variety.'[19] As we work the Steps, our spirituality, however

---

[19] Attributed to psychologist William James in A.A.'s second Appendix, "Spiritual Experience." William James wrote *The Varieties of Spiritual Experience*, a book, reprint published by Modern Library. This book, although anything but an easy read, can be worth the struggle. This book had a great influence on Bill W.

we define it, gradually expands. Thus the spiritual awakening is not so much a goal as an ongoing process.

Actually, it is this awakening that is never-ending rather than recovery. It is also this spiritual awakening that empowers us.

The shift from admitting the powerlessness of the addiction/dysfunction to reclaiming personal power is accomplished because the 12 Steps address four major themes necessary for effective, continuing spiritual and personal growth:

- discipline,
- self-examination and confession,
- reaching out to others, and,
- the willingness to change.

Before we examine each theme individually, it's well worth noting that each theme is interwoven with all the others, and that each is as important as all the others. Taken together, they form the whole. Although any one may take on more importance for a time, this is only temporary, and eventually all four come equally into play.

Discipline

'Discipline' is another often misunderstood word. Although its Latin root means *training* or *instruction*, we tend to associate the word only with punishment and self-denial. While there can be some teaching value in punishment – it can teach us NOT to do something – there is far more to training and instruction than the 'thou shall nots.'

In general, we think of teaching as helping people learn how to do something like a job skill or how to get in touch with feelings or how to alter behavior in positive ways. It's interesting that the root of teaching's corollary, 'education,' may actually be *to draw out of.*

At its best, teaching brings out the best in both teacher and student.

Understood in their fullest sense, 12 Step Programs aim to teach, or educate us how to let go of our addiction/dysfunction and draw out of us the ability to live a full, productive, spiritual life.

Of course, 'discipline' also implies practice. And like any other skill, practice takes some time.

Probably the first training or discipline we hear when we come to a 12 Step meeting is *keep coming back.* It is recognized that regular attendance at meetings both increases our opportunity to learn about ourselves and our new way of life, and works to help us change the structure of our living patterns to new, positive patterns. Indeed, regular attendance at 12 Step meetings is a form of self-discipline. We take in the suggestion to *keep coming back* and turn it into self-discipline, the powerful action of regular attendance.

Equally important, and equally a matter of powerful, disciplined action, is the admonition to quit practicing our addiction/dysfunction *one day at a time.* This too creates new behavior patterns and gives us measurable success.

This sort of learning and self-discipline continues as we work through the Steps and integrate the principles of the Program in our daily living. Each time we take a Step we are acting powerfully on our own behalf. Every time we remember one of the principles and use it, we are practicing the discipline of the Program.

There is, of course, the more negative discipline of a slip as well. Although fear of a return to the addiction/dysfunction is certainly a real threat in the beginning of recovery, as we saw earlier, this danger will drop away. But even this fear can be used positively as long as we need it.

Self-Examination And Confession

Self-examination, and the resulting self-knowledge, is critically important to our recovery. It is also a critically important component of all spiritual disciplines. Without it, we are apt to continue to twist in the wind, repeating old mistakes and blaming others for them.

Twelve Steppers have already begun this self-examination when they get to Program. If we hadn't, we would never reach the acceptance of our problem that allows us to take powerful action and ask for help in the first place.

Once in Program, we find self-examination a continuing theme. The 12 Steps, coupled with the Fellowship of the group, allow this self-examination to proceed without becoming maudlin mental masturbation, for self-searching is not performed in isolation.

The 4th Step, *Made a searching and fearless moral inventory of ourselves,* is, of course, the first major effort we make at formal self-examination. The theme is continued in the 8th Step, and again in the 10th Step, but not until we get a reality check through Step 5.

Step 5, *Admitted to God, to ourselves, and to another human being the exact nature of our wrongs*, is a major part of 12 Step self-searching. This step allows us to tell our story safely to one other person. Often we are telling this person things we would never have dreamed of confessing to another. We discover, to our relief, that we are not judged, simply heard. Often the people we are talking with are able to share something similar in their own background. As a result, we discover that maybe we aren't quite as bad as we thought – a little bit of sanity is restored.

The listener also often asks the questions that either reveal parts of our story that we left out, or shows us that we aren't as different as we thought. Note too, that Step 5 also involves reaching out to others, one of the keys to a spiritual awakening.

Step 8, *Made a list of all people we had harmed and became willing to make amends to them all,* takes even more self-examination. By this time, because of the work we've done, we begin to have a real understanding of our past. Actually writing down a list of the people we've harmed is the beginning of our willingness to make amends. Willingness to take corrective action through amends is the beginning of our taking personal responsibility for our actions.

Personal responsibility becomes more than theoretical in the 9th Step, *Made direct amends to such people whenever possible, except when to do so would injure them or others.* Note that the Step calls for us to make direct amends even if we face some 'injury.' There can be no denying the power in these Steps, both for ourselves and for others.

By the time we reach Step 10, *Continued to take personal inventory and when we were wrong promptly admitted it,* some balance has been restored and we begin to see the positive aspects of ourselves because we've been able to look squarely at the negative we worked so hard to avoid. Here, in the *12 and 12* we are urged to also look at what we've done well.[20] The balance we are seeking includes acceptance of what works well in our lives as well as what doesn't work.

As constructive self-examination becomes a habit, we discover we are able to bring discipline to our practice of the 12 Steps, and this practice makes it possible for us to grow – to make better decisions, to be more honest with ourselves about motivations and to take more powerful actions.

Reaching Out To Others

Until the 12th Step, the reaching out we've done has usually been by asking for help and/or understanding. This has had

---

[20] *A.A.,* p. 569

the effect of breaking up isolation and giving us a more balanced perspective on our own lives.

In the 12th Step, Having had a spiritual awakening as a result of these steps, we tried to carry this message to alcoholics[21] and to practice these principles in all our affairs, we offer help to others who want help. Because of our experience with the 12 Steps we now have a message to carry.

This willingness to be of service moves us into the larger world – the world that our addiction/dysfunction had led us to effectively reject.

Twelve Steppers tend to downplay this sort of offer to help, emphasizing that we do it for selfish reasons, *to keep us free from practicing our addiction/dysfunction* or *to keep our memory green.* And although these are certainly some of the reasons, they're not the only ones. For being able to help is truly empowering. It's silly not to recognize this.

Of course, we began reaching out to others when we first came to our 12 Step Program. Every time we speak or listen to another, we are reaching out. Steps 5, 9, and 10 include reaching out. Reaching out is also a recurring theme.

Those who practice all 12 Steps are people who have begun to practice an effective self-discipline, including self-examination, because they are willing to change and to involve others in their process. As a result they become people who are able to take constructive action on their own behalf and on the behalf of others. In other words, they have become truly powerful people.

One Mystery Solved

If the kids were involved in a sport or visiting with their father on Saturdays, I'd usually go to an 11 a.m. meeting at the club. It was a closed discussion with some

---

[21] Name your addiction here.

old-timers as well as newcomers and those of us in between.

Although I had worked the Steps and was fairly firm in my sobriety – I had about four years at this point – I often struggled with the concept of letting go absolutely. Oh, not about drinking and using, but about the other aspects of my life like love, or as I came to call them, 'Big R Relationships.' I never wanted to talk about letting go at this meeting, however. And Old Fred was the reason.

Old Fred probably wasn't that old, but he had been sober for a long time. And one of his favorite things to talk about was acceptance.

"Acceptance is the answer," he'd almost shout, sometimes pounding the table with each word. "Whatever the problem, when you finally accept what's going on, *of its own action it will change!*"

He'd go on to explain that you couldn't accept something in hope it would change – that was cheating. You had to accept whatever it was just the way it was, with no doubt, no holding back, no hope of change.

Of course, I thought he was making no sense whatsoever. Actually, I hoped he'd either shut-up on the subject or quit coming to that meeting.

Apparently, however, his words worked their way into my subconscious, for I found myself occasionally asking for acceptance of whatever situation I was in that was making me unhappy. Much to my disappointment, it worked! When I asked with sincerity, acceptance was given to me and when it was, the situation would, of its own action, change. Sometimes I didn't like the change, other times I hardly noticed.

Eventually I came to understand that before I can 'let go and let God,' I have to reach the acceptance Fred talked about.

Willingness To Change

Implicit in discipline, self-examination and reaching out to others, is the willingness to change. It is the magic ingredient that makes the Steps really work.

This willingness shows up in all sorts of ways in 12 Step practice – from postponing acting out our addiction/dysfunction for 24 hours or less at a time, to the discipline of coming to meetings and working the Steps, to our desire to reach out to others and try and help. Indeed, the *12 and 12* tells us in Step 3 that willingness is the key to the practice of the Steps.[22]

Willingness also includes the willingness to believe in some sort of Power greater than ourselves. Again, it's important to notice that we are not told what to believe, just that we must become willing.

This vital, spiritual discipline is necessary because much of what we learn in the initial self-examination is that we don't know how to change. We've tried will power and tricks to no avail. The self-examination reveals the futility of these methods and we come to accept that, by ourselves, not much change will happen.

That necessary deflation of egomania[23] allows us to look beyond ourselves, to see that our addiction is, in a very real sense, more powerful than we are. Quickly, or slowly, we are able to make the leap into faith that allows real healing and change to take place – as long as we are willing.

Again, we are taking powerful action on our own behalf.

We Are Worthy and Deserving

No one who comes to a 12 Step Program has a balanced view of themselves. Lack of self-worth is a major component in any addiction/dysfunction.

The 12 Steps help us begin to get a realistic look at ourselves and, in time, we come to believe that we do have a right to be here, just as those around us do. We begin to

---

[22] *12 and 12*, p. 93

[23] Egomania' is not synonymous with 'ego.' We need an ego, a sense of self, to get along in the world; egomania is defined as "self-centered, selfish."

recognize that we are indeed worthy and deserving – not of riches and fame – but of being one among many, deserving of being treated decently and with respect and acknowledgment.

As we come to see ourselves with more balance, we are able to see others with less judgment.

But this self-acceptance doesn't come quickly or easily. Self-denigration is a tough habit to break, and the Fellowship's insistence on perpetual powerlessness and never-ending recovery doesn't make it any easier.

Instead of acknowledgment for success, we're often encouraged to be careful. Instead of praise for what we've done right, we're often admonished not to take any credit at all. It's as if we're allowed to go only so far with our recovery and no further.

Part of this stems from our left-over, internal belief that somehow we are wrong. Even as we begin to change our view of ourselves for the better, the echo of that belief often leads us to actually fear our own power. In meetings we not only hear the echo of our own fear, but that of those around us.

But, as outlined in the Promises, the Program is designed to give us much more. As we grasp the fuller consequences of the 12 Steps, we learn that we truly are deserving; we come to trust ourselves and finally, recognize that we are both recovered and empowered.

Chapter 5

Of Inventories, Confessions, Amends And Self-Worth

Guilt is really the reverse side of the coin of pride. Guilt aims at self-destruction, and pride aims at the destruction of others. (p. 140)

Self-examination, self-disclosure, and amends are powerful tools for spiritual and personal growth. Steps 4, and 8 are the inventory steps. It is here that we begin to get an honest look at how we've been wrong, both in our attitudes and in our actions, particularly in our actions toward other people. Although we begin self-disclosure when we admit to our addiction/dysfunction in a meeting, it is in Step 5 that it becomes rigorous. It's in Step 5 that we actually tell another person about the shortcomings we uncovered in Step 4.

In Step 6 we again look deeply within to find the willingness for change and in Step 7 we ask the God of our understanding for help in making those changes. Step 9 moves us toward action when it comes to taking personal responsibility as we apologize and, if necessary, make restitution to those people we've hurt.

When, however, these Steps are combined with the myths of never-ending recovery and perpetual powerlessness, they can become tools of unnecessary guilt, and self-flagellation. Then, instead of moving us toward the balance and freedom the Program offers, we risk worsening self-worth and even depression. Pushed to extremes, this could add up to a slip – precisely what we're working to avoid.

Building A New Life

One way to look at the 12 Steps is to see the first nine as the creation of a the foundation for a new life, while the last three are the tools used to maintain that new life. If, however, we believe we can never become recovered and that we must remain perpetually powerless, we never complete laying the foundation. Unless we let go of the myths, we tend to try and rebuild the foundation over and over again, rather than continuing with the rest of the structure.

A major portion of the foundation building of a new life is in the 4th Step – the taking of a moral inventory. When this is done, as the Step says, 'thoroughly,' it sets the stage for the rest of the Steps. But if we believe our recovery is never-ending, we are tempted to repeat the 4th Step multiple times.

The Problem With Multiple 4th Steps

The problem with multiple 4th Steps is one of emphasis. On the surface, more than one 4th may look like a good idea. After all, it is reasoned, no matter how thorough and honest we try to be the first time around, we are apt to miss some things. Not only that, but as we live life, new issues come up.

But re-doing 4th Steps puts the emphasis on the negative. For our 'wrongs' or 'character defects' are exactly what's emphasized in the 4th Step in both the *Big Book* and the *12 and 12*. If we keep looking at what's wrong, we'll never get to what's right, or to the balanced view of ourselves that's called for in the 10th Step.

Annual 4th Steps

This is also true for the growing custom of so-called Annual 4th Steps. At first glance, an Annual 4th isn't so different, in some ways, than the goal setting that goes on around Jan. 1st every year. The idea is to provide a frame for an annual personal evaluation, but because it's called a 4th Step, there is a real tendency to look only at what's wrong.

While no one would deny that, when we come into Program, we must look at the wrongs; once we've done a thorough job, it's time to move on. Always looking at what's wrong is far from a balanced view, and balance is integral to a becoming powerfully recovered.

A wise friend with many years in successful 12 Step work puts it this way:

> The 4th Step is like getting ready to plant a garden. You go in and dig the soil, pulling as many weeds as you can find. Then you plant. As the plants grow, particularly when they are young, so do the weeds you missed. The 10th Step is for the weeds we missed and the new ones that come along. But if we've done a good job with the original preparation, we will never have as many weeds again.

It is the 10th Step that helps us move toward balance, but before we leave the multiple 4th Steps, let's look a bit more deeply.

Of course, multiple 4th Steps also implies multiple 5th Steps. Again, the problem here is the emphasis – it's almost always on the negative rather than on a balanced view of the self.

There is a world of difference between a formal 5th Step, and a quiet discussion with a friend or therapist that can come when, after we've made some progress, we recognize that we're drifting off track. While many of us make a habit of having one or two people in our lives from whom we have no secrets, there's rarely any reason at all to re-do the work we did in our original 5th Step.

If we're going to work multiple 4th and 5th Steps, what about multiple 6th and 7 Steps?

Multiple 6th And 7th Steps Are Problems Too

Becoming willing for our lives to change is a powerful action, as is asking a God of our understanding for help with those changes. For some, these are the two most difficult Steps of all. When we first came to program, ridding ourselves of our addiction/dysfunction had an immediacy to it. Many of us thought it would be fairly simple.

Now, with Step 6, we're asked to become willing to let go at an even deeper level – down where many of our problems really begin. It is here where doubt about the Program and ourselves really begins to surface.

Some doubt that they are worthy of the changes they are asking for; others discover a stubborn streak, usually masking fear, they had no idea was there. Implicit in this struggle is the actual thoughtful acceptance of who we truly are – a subject we had avoided for years.

This is followed by the need to find some true humility to work Step 7. Not only do we have to come to some sort of terms with a Power greater than ourselves, we have to let go of our illusion of control and ask that Power for help.

What, in Step 3, had been a simple willingness to believe in something, has now become a test of our willingness to find a faith that works.

Steps 6 and 7 are meant to be foundation Steps. Once we become willing to change, willing to accept and let go of our defects, we are, by and large, given the willingness. The same can be said for asking the God of our understanding to remove those deficiencies.

If we insist on repeating these Steps over and over again because we've done multiple 4th Steps, our emphasis is still on the wrongs, not on balance. This actually becomes a re-doing of work we've already done. This sort of unnecessary repeating could be called a lack of faith. It also can act as a way to avoid moving forward.

This is not to say, of course, that as we move through our days we are immune from having problems with our attitudes and our actions. We certainly don't lose our humanity because we've completed some or all of the Steps. And part of being human is making mistakes.

There's also the very real chance that we will have omitted something important in our original 4th Step. But as long as it wasn't deliberate, it can be handled with the 10th Step.

The 10th Step

The 10th Step is the first of the so-called maintenance steps. It is designed to help us monitor our attitudes and behaviors in our day-to-day life. But there's a huge difference in emphasis in the 10th Step. Take a close look:

> Continued to take personal inventory and *when* we were wrong, promptly admitted it. (Emphasis mine.)

I've emphasized 'when' because it's important. Implicit in Step 10 is the fact that we are not *always* wrong.

We Are Not Always Wrong!

There is a tendency among most addicts, whether the addiction is to a behavior or to a substance, to believe we are always wrong. This lack of self-worth shows up in a lot of different ways including always apologizing, refusing compliments, not daring to try new things for fear of failure – the list can go on and on.

The 10th Step allows us to see these and other patterns, but also urges us to take credit for what we do well. In fact, the *12 and 12*'s 10th Step text admonishes us that our inventory isn't to be taken only in red ink.[24] We are to look at the positive as well as the negative and all the stuff in the middle. The 10th Step is really about developing ongoing self-acceptance and gentle self-correction.

We are, of course, told to promptly admit when we are wrong. While this might include talking a problem over with someone else, it doesn't have the formality of the 5th Step. It is assumed we won't let things build, but will handle them more or less as they occur. By this time we've gotten some judgment about ourselves, and some practice with self-honesty.

Implicit in the 10th Step, and the rest of the maintenance steps, 11 and 12, is a continuing and deepening of the faith that originally allowed us to work Steps 6 and 7.

What About BIG Problems

Occasionally we will discover, along the way, a pattern or create a problem that seems to require more than just a 10th Step. In my case, the issue was money. At around 6 years I realized that although I had made progress in many areas, my behavior around money was truly destructive. This is when I joined DA. Although I did do 4th Step-like work in this area – that is, I looked hard and long at my attitudes and behaviors around money – I was able to bring some balance to myself by calling it more 10th Step work.

I did talk over this inventory with someone in Program, and it resembled a 5th Step, except I was able to take more credit for what I had done right. The result was a faster healing.

Amends

The 9th Step is designed to let us clear the decks of the past. It is here that we use the information we gathered about

---

[24] *12 and 12*, p. 93

ourselves in the 4th and 8th and take personal responsibility by going to each person on our list and apologizing. When we're done, we can let the past go. We no longer have to suffer the guilt for all that's been undone or done poorly. We indeed have laid a foundation for a new beginning. If we keep re-doing Steps we'll never get there.

Let's face it, amends or a simple apology work best when offered as soon as the event we want to apologize for takes place. When we develop the habit of the 10th Step it's fairly easy to make an expression of regret in the moment, or at least close to the moment.

Of course, we're not talking about constant apology. You know what I mean. The person who apologizes for everything is as out of balance as the person who never admits a mistake. The key is taking responsibility when we offend.

Amends are one thing, constant apology is another – lack of self-worth can show up in the refusal of a compliment, the way we put a resume together and our posture. But these issues can, and should be handled through additional 10th Step work.

Group-think

The first time I heard someone state they had no friends who weren't in Program I hadn't been sober long and it sounded reasonable, even desirable. Over time, I heard this sort of statement again and again, often from someone with years on the Program. I even adopted part of the idea myself for a while, by refusing to date anyone who wasn't also a recovering alcoholic or addict.

It wasn't until I was 10 years clean and sober that it really dawned on me what a shame this sort of thinking actually is. By this time I had friends in and out of Program and enjoyed them all, but I hadn't thought about it much.

When I moved to a new area, it took me a while to get to a woman's meeting. It was one of those meetings where people announce how long they've been sober when they introduce themselves, and I was pleasantly surprised to find that several of the women had much more time than I did.

My pleasure turned sour, however, at the response they gave to a newcomer who was feeling awkward at work. To a woman, the old-timers told her over and over again that it was impossible to get along with 'normies.' One way or another they stated that 'normies' were different and that although we couldn't avoid them entirely, we needed to restrict our friendships to those in 12 Step groups.

Finally I raised my hand, reminded them that I had 10 years, and stated that I found many 'normies' both understanding and a whole lot of fun as well. I went on to outline my belief that true sobriety embodies the ability to move freely in the world, which includes people of all sorts, not just those who participate in a 12 Step group.

I may have been a bit strident. I know I quoted liberally from the *Big Book* and the *12 and 12*. I also know it's the only time I've spoken at a meeting where no one even said 'hello' or introduced themselves after the meeting. As I drove away, I realized that this group had formed a dogma all their own. Needless to say, I never went back.

The Dangers Of Group-Think

'Group-think' can be defined in a variety of ways. One of my favorites is to think of it as peer pressure. The thing to realize is that this sort of pressure isn't always overt. We receive subtle clues from those around us all the time – clues that let us know if we are liked or disliked, approved of or not.

When we come to a 12 Step Program we are particularly vulnerable to this kind of subtle (and usually unconscious) coercion. We look around and see people who are feeling much better than we are. We listen to their stories and try to discover how they do it.

This is why the myths of perpetual powerlessness and never-ending recovery are so pervasive. In the beginning we don't know enough to question what we're hearing; if we do, our questions are often pushed aside with a warning of one sort or another.

After a while, we've heard the myths so often, we don't recognize them as such. They've become part of our own consciousness and we believe them to be true. If someone does come along and, for example, introduce themselves as recover*ed*, there is likely to be an outcry of horror at the meeting. At least a couple of people will recount how they slipped because they thought they were cured. Someone is likely to warn about the dangers of pride.

If someone suggests they feel powerful, much the same thing happens. They are warned, one way or another that they are treading on dangerous ground.

It's not surprising that these myths never get questioned.

But there's danger in groupthink. It is, after all, individuals who have new ideas. Insightful thinking is impossible if one depends only on what others say.

I'm always amused when someone at a meeting says: *It was your best thinking that got you here!* The implication is that our thinking must have been pretty awful or we wouldn't have ended up in a 12 Step Program. Of course, many of us find the benefits so great that we wouldn't give up any of the experiences that got us where we are. Which, to my mind anyway, may mean that as muddled as my thinking was that got me here, it turned out to be pretty darn good!

Alcoholics Anonymous recognized that groupthink could stifle clear thinking and made an effort to mitigate the problem. Although, at the General Service level, A.A. is a democracy, it doesn't run by a simple majority. Instead, the bylaws recognize the 'substantial minority' When an issue comes up and some feel that the majority of the Board or Conference is headed in the wrong direction, the issue is tabled. It is brought up again at the next session and, if need be, the next and the next.

Often the vote swings to the former minorities' side. It is exactly this way, although in less formal fashion, that the phrase *as we understand God* came to be added to A.A. literature. A few, led by Jim B., felt adding the phrase would open the Program up for more people. After a while, the rest agreed. The addition of that phrase has been one of the more important reasons the Program has spread as far as it has.

Because the myths of perpetual powerlessness and never-ending recovery are myths – that is, they can't be supported by the original literature, it's highly unlikely that A.A. or any other 12 Step Group will ever make any official statement about them, which is probably the way it should be.

Instead, it is up to us, the members, to let go of the myths individually. As more and more do let go, the new thinking will gradually be reflected in the Fellowship and the needed changes will take place automatically. People will become comfortable recognizing, and saying, they are recovered. Those who are successful in the world won't be made to feel their recovery is somehow in jeopardy. Feelings of being a victim of our addiction will fall away as we empower ourselves by taking responsibility. Newcomers will be less resistant and the poor, who know powerlessness at a level most of us do not, will feel welcome. Our spirits will soar as our spirituality grows, free from constraint.

Letting go of the myths of never-ending recovery and perpetual powerlessness may take us further than we can even imagine.

Chapter 6

Powerfully Recovered And Your Program

...We shall have to try for all the freedom from fear that is possible for us to attain ...(p. 61)

N ot surprisingly, the possibility of becoming powerfully recovered brings up a number of important questions, including:

*   How can I know if I'm recovered?
*   What about newcomers – aren't these ideas risky for them?
*   How can I be sure I'm using my power in the 'right' way?
*   What do I say to those who think I'm risking a slip by claiming to be powerfully recovered?

Each question is important at one time or another.

How Can I Know If I'm Recovered?

There is only one person who can decide if you're recovered or not – you! It's as a personal decision as the one you made about having an addiction/dysfunction in the first place. Like accepting an addiction/dysfunction, there is no 'test' or exact method to know for sure.

Seven Questions

There are, however, seven questions you can ask yourself, that will help you know what is true for you. Use these as a guide, always remembering that they are not set in stone, and that ultimately, you are responsible.

1. **Why do you want to consider yourself powerfully recovered?**

Whenever we fly in the face of convention, it's worth taking some time to examine our motivations. There can be problems with egomania, or a desire to 'graduate,' or an urge to be 'better than' others. None of these are valid reasons; on the contrary, such an attitude will only lead to trouble.

It helps to remember that there is no competition when it comes to working a 12 Step Program. The bottom line is *always* abstinence. Besides, there's no 'prize' or 'badge' to 'win' in 12 Step work.

Personal growth ideally is a life-time project. It happens when we're paying attention and taking action to make our lives more effective, enjoyable, and honest.

Most of the members I know who feel comfortable claiming to be powerfully recovered report that they grew into this position. It happened gradually. Many hadn't even labeled what they felt, but recognized it when I asked. It may be that this evolutionary approach is the best one. A gentle recognition that it has become true is much better than straining toward a goal that is impossible to define exactly.

2. **Do you long to practice your addiction/dysfunction?**

If you do, you can't claim to be recovered. There's no question that abstinence is a must if you are to be powerfully recovered. The person who still longs to yield to their addiction/dysfunction, is involved in recovery, but is not yet recover*ed*. The same is true for the person who thinks they can learn to practice their addiction/dysfunction in some moderate or 'normal' fashion.

To be recovered, you must not only have accepted that you are addicted, but, through the Steps, moved beyond your addiction/dysfunction. The *Big Book* puts it this way in the Promises when it says:

> We will seldom be interested in (our addiction/dysfunction). If tempted, we

recoil from it as from a hot flame. We
react sanely and normally, and we will find
that this has happened automatically. (A.A.
pp. 84-85)

This change in attitude and thinking from the insanity of
practicing or wanting to practice our addiction/dysfunction to
no longer being interested in it, is true freedom. When we
can say this is real for us, and say it with honesty and with
humility, we can truly claim to be recovered.

3.   Have you thoroughly completed all 12 of the Steps?

It takes all 12 Steps to reap the full benefits of the
Program, and until we've completed each one, as it is
written, we cannot claim to be recover*ed*. For it is through
the practice of all 12 of the Steps that we will be given the
freedom from our addiction/dysfunction the Program
promises.

It's important to note, however, that completion of the
12 Steps doesn't guarantee we will be recover*ed*. It's
possible to work all the 12 Steps and still be on shaky
ground. This seems to be simply a function of time. It takes
time to rid our bodies of the physical aspects of our
addiction/dysfunction; it also takes time to change the habits
of thought that contributed to our old patterns.

However, when time is combined with the rigorous
practice of the Steps, the freedom will come. How much
time is impossible to say; what can be said, however, is that
the knowledge of becoming recovered will be felt by the
individual when the time is right.

4.   Have you developed a way to continue honest self-searching?

The 10th Step, *Continued to take personal inventory
and when we were wrong promptly admitted it,* provides a
way for us to continue self-examination. For it is through
self-examination that we stay aware of what we're about –

on a day-to-day basis. It is here, however we do it, that we also have the opportunity to see what we're doing well, where we need improvement, and pick up any danger points.

The form of this practice is highly individual. Some take a few minutes at the end of the day to review; others have come to trust their inner voice to let them know when they are off course. Some use a combination of methods. However we do it, it must become an integral part of our lives.

5. **Do you have some sort of understanding and relationship with a Power greater than yourself?**

Such an understanding certainly doesn't have to be 'God' or any particular form. But it does seem that we do better if we have some sense of connection with the whole. Some return to the church they grew up in; others find a different church. Still others don't go to church at all, but develop their own spiritual practices.

One thing to keep in mind when working in this area, is that many find their conception and relationship with the God of their understanding changing. Unless the change recreates the desire to practice the addiction/dysfunction, it's OK. Growth and change are part of the process too.

6. **Are you willing to reach out to others and share what you've learned?**

We can't afford to be selfish and expect either to become or stay recovered. How we reach out will vary from person to person and from time-to-time. Obviously we can't ignore our responsibilities to perform service.

Stints in 12 Step service definitely help our own recovery, and helps move us toward becoming recovered. As we grow and change, we may find our reaching out taking other forms, either within the 12 Step community or elsewhere. Staying willing to be of service, whatever form that takes, is part of being powerfully recovered.

Not Always My Hand

For many years I was involved in 12-Step work – my name was listed with our Central Office and when I got a call I went.

I also served not only as coffee maker but as secretary and even treasurer for several groups. I took meetings into hospitals and was GSR for a year. I was even on the speaker's circuit for a short time and in a minor way.

Each experience was truly valuable and I'm glad I did each one.

However, there came a time when the obligations I'd acquired began to weigh heavy and I felt some resentment building. I talked to a woman I trusted who had much more sobriety than I and who knew me quite well.

"Maybe," she said, "it's time for you to step back and let some of the newcomers have a chance at service."

"But what about my responsibility that the hand of A.A. always be there," I asked.

"Yes," she said with a wise twinkle, "we're always responsible that the hand be there, but the hand doesn't always have to be our own."

I must have looked confused, for she went on. "You don't have to do all the work yourself. You've been sober long enough so you're setting an example, even if you don't make the coffee. That quiet example is an important part of making sure someone's hand is always there."

7. **If you claim to be powerfully recovered and the claim isn't working, are you willing to let it go?**

It's absolutely critical that we stay honest with ourselves, and this includes honesty about being powerfully recover*ed* It may well be that you find your claim to being powerfully recover*ed* is premature. The protection against problems in this area is to stay willing to admit you were mistaken and go back to the concept of being in recovery.

I do know that my own journey, and the journey of others has sometimes meant letting go of either empowerment or being recovered, or both. It hasn't happened in many years, but as I was beginning to explore these ideas, I had to back off them a number of times and get back to the basics of the 12 Steps.

Each time, the very act of going back to basics was an act of power – and, over time, I became more empowered. Finally I came to trust that, as long as I keep to my path, I'm unlikely to drink alcohol or misuse drugs again. I do, however, keep track through a variety of self-searching techniques, for I never want to return to the practice of my addiction/dysfunctions again. It's all part of my spiritual discipline. I do claim I'm recovered; I don't claim I'm immune from a slip.

Although most come to a sense of being recovered gradually, occasionally someone tries to make the decision prematurely – only to find they are uncomfortable and tempted back to their addiction/dysfunction. The trick is, not surprisingly, to be *willing* to step back and do some more homework.

Aren't There Risks For Newcomers?

Some express real concern about newcomers hearing, and misunderstanding, a claim of being powerfully recovered. The argument runs something like this:

> A newcomer might think they can become cured or learn how to return to their addiction/dysfunction, or they may get caught up in power and have a slip – it's better to keep them feeling powerless and believing that their recovery will be never-ending.

I don't agree. When I look back on my early recovery I know things were said that were potentially damaging, but since I was willing to go to any lengths to get sober, I wasn't harmed. I've seen the same thing over and over again since. A willing newcomer seems to operate in a 'zone of protection' until they have a chance to get their feet on the ground a bit.

Even if that weren't the case, I don't believe anyone is ever harmed by the truth. Far better to have a truthful goal like powerful recovery, than to risk being mired down in the myths of never-ending recovery and perpetual powerlessness.

While fear is indeed a motivator in early recovery, people don't stay in a Program only because of fear. Gradually they learn that a much more positive outlook is possible. To insist anyone stay afraid is to deny them the Promises.

How Can I Know I'm Using Power Well?

Like so many things in life, there is no guarantee we will use our empowerment in exactly the right way. There are some risks. We make mistakes – it's part of being human. The trick is to stay honest with ourselves, about what we're doing, what our motivation is, and what results we're looking for.

As long as we're willing to make changes and corrections, we're safe. This is another reason the habit of the 10th Step is so important.

What Do I Say To Others?

This is really a question about how to fly in the face of conventional 12 Step thinking. Although you will develop your own style, there are some guidelines that may be helpful.

You Don't Need To Convert Anyone To Your Beliefs

If you decide you are powerfully recovered, or that you want to work toward that goal – fine. Such decisions do not require you to try and convince anyone else to do the same. In fact, to do so might be an indication more homework is needed. I find the only times I really try to convert someone to my point of view are the times I'm not sure of my own ground.

On the other hand, you certainly don't need to hide your decision either.

No One Can Effectively Argue With Your Experience

There's no denying that if you tell someone, or a meeting that you're feeling powerfully recovered, you'll probably get some argument, maybe even lots of it. If, however, you share those feeling in the frame of your own experience, you may get less resistance than you expect. In fact, you may be delightfully surprised to find others who have been sensing the same thing but have been afraid to even ask the question.

When you do get resistance, there's simply no point in arguing – no one can effectively argue with your experience anyway. They may try, but your experience is your experience, and anyone who tells you that you don't really feel that way is speaking from their own confusion and fear. Frankly, they have no right!

Pick your times carefully, when you're feeling strong and when you're feeling safe. Ask the God of your understanding for guidance, and trust your intuition.

What About Sponsorship?

There are two issues here. One is likely to be your own sponsor. If you have a sponsor who disagrees with your decision, you need to handle the situation with love and honesty. It goes almost without saying that you should listen carefully to what they have to say. You may find that, at least at this point in time, they're right. However, they may not be. Sponsors are no more immune from the myths or making mistakes than anyone else.

It may help to remember that sponsorship is not a lifetime contract. It's OK to fire a sponsor, provided you've looked deeply and honestly within yourself before you do so. Although it's best to do this gently and with a careful, non-judgmental discussion of your position, it doesn't always work that way. It may be that all you need to say is something like: this relationship is no longer working for me.

The other part of the equation is when you're sponsoring someone else. The best sort of sponsoring comes from a simple sharing of our own experience. All you can do is tell your 'baby' or 'sponsee' how you feel and, if it's called for, how you came to feel this way.

Remember, on this and other issues, at most you're setting up a goal or a model. You can't force anyone into any particular position. Remember too, you are not responsible *for* their actions. Your responsibility is *to* them.

The Rewards

What might it be like if you actually became powerfully recovered? What would you do differently? How would you feel? Would the Promises be more likely to come true for you? Would you feel more effective, and serene, in your life?

Only you can answer these questions – and they are worth considering.

What rewards have I experienced? There's no one answer to that, but one of the ways I like to express it is that my skin fits better. I'm more accepting of myself, all of my self.

It seems the more accepting I am of all of myself, the easier it is to see the wonderful whole of others.

I'm more willing to look deeply, beyond the surface. I'm more apt to congratulate myself for a job well done, and

I'm less likely to beat myself up when I do something wrong or that doesn't work. I also recognize that much of what I do is in the middle – very average, even boring.

Today I am much more willing to risk to pursue my dreams and ideas. I don't deny my effectiveness or feel I'm not good enough to try. Generally, life is better, more fun, more interesting – the promises have come true for me, and they keep coming true, at ever deepening levels.

Your outcomes will be different, but they may surprise you with the sense of freedom and at-one-ness you feel.

Chapter 7

Powerfully Recovered And The Principle Of Attraction

The essence of all growth is a willingness to change for the better and then an unremitting willingness to shoulder whatever responsibility this entails. (p. 115)

W hen I came into A.A. over twenty years ago, there were significantly fewer women than men and even fewer people of color. Unfortunately, the same is true today.

A.A. collects statistics about gender and ethnicity every 2 years when they survey a representative percentage of registered groups. This survey is considered part of A.A.'s regular inventory. The goal of the survey is to find ways of improving their outreach effectiveness.

The table below indicates the percentage of various groups in the general U.S. population and A.A.'s 1998 membership survey for the same groups.[25]

The accuracy of statistics, of course, depends on how they are collected and the results are always subject to interpretation. For example, the National Institute on Alcohol Abuse and Alcoholism (NIAAA)[26] has research on

---

[25] I've used only A.A.'s statistics in the U.S. because they are the easiest to find. My experience, which is mostly limited to the U.S., indicates that the racial and gender makeup up is roughly the same with most other 12 Step groups.

AA's statistics come from the pamphlet *Alcoholics Anonymous 1998 Membership* Survey, which is available through the General Service office and most Central and Intergroup offices. General Population numbers come from the U.S. Census Bureau web site: http://www.census.gov/population/estimates/nation/intfile3-1.txt

[26] The information referenced here comes from the NIAAA surveys conducted in 1984; their web site is: http://www.niaaa.nih.gov

alcoholism for both race and gender. All sorts of interesting
things pop up.

	Percent of General Population	Percent of AA Population
White	82.2%	88%
Black	12.8%	5%
Hispanic	11.8%	4%
Native American	0.9%	2%
Asian	4.1%	1%
Female	51%	34%

One survey indicates Blacks have both a higher
percentage of their population that never drinks, and a higher
percentage of alcoholism. Another states women have a
lower incidence of alcoholism than men, then goes on to say
there are more alcoholics among younger women which
might indicate the percentage is increasing.

However, these numbers are based largely on discharges
from hospitals, and since we don't even approach universal
access to medical care in this country, it's difficult to know
exactly what they mean. Coupled with the fact that many
come to 12 Step groups dealing with chemical addiction
without any hospitalization, this information results in even
more confusion.

It is possible, however, to draw the general conclusion
that Alcoholics Anonymous is largely a white, male
organization. There's no reason to expect the rest of the 12
Step movement to be much different – except in Al-Anon,
CODA, OA and ACoA. We'll look at these exceptions in a
moment.

It would also be completely unreasonable to assume that white men are significantly more likely to be alcoholic than men of color. It also doesn't seem reasonable that women are more likely to be immune from alcoholism than men.

We need to look for another explanation for the reasons the make-up of 12 Step groups fail to reflect the gender and racial mix of the general population more closely.

12 Step Groups Reflect Society, Not Need

Not surprisingly, 12 Step groups reflect our culture rather than the need for recovery within our culture.

One way to define culture is to say it means the way our society works day-by-day. It's the context of our lives, which is difficult to see because we're in the midst of it. Our culture includes what we watch on TV, the news we see and hear, the movies we watch, the way we interact with people at work and at play. It includes what and who we expect to see, how we expect to be and are treated, and how we automatically treat and think about others.

And white men dominate our culture. In spite of the civil rights movement and affirmative action, white men have most of the power in this society. Stay with me here – this is not a popular idea, largely because it's invisible.

We only have to look at a few facts to see this is true, including:

* women receive approximately 72¢ for every $1.00 men earn for comparable work,[27]
* white men run most of the corporations, and,
* white men make up by far the largest percentage of elected officials.

---

[27] National Committee on Pay Equity, 1999:
http://www.feminist.com/fairpay/f_change.htm

Yes, there are exceptions; no, not all white men have power. It's not men's 'fault. All men are not wrong or bad or deliberately, consciously trying to oppress others. But take a moment and look at our images of power; if you're honest I think you'll see that our perceptions of power are centered on white men.

Usually women are quicker to see this because, regrettably, women have less power than men. Lots of men, however, experience lack of power as well and come to see that equal opportunity is still a goal we haven't yet reached.

Simply, and emphatically put, people of color and women have less power than white men.

What About Al-Anon, CODA, OA And Acoa?

Al-Anon, CODA (Co-Dependents Anonymous), OA (Overeaters Anonymous) and ACoA (Adult Children of Alcoholics) all have more women than men. Again, this reflects our society.

Since there are more men in A.A. and since Al-Anon is set up to help the families of Alcoholics, it's not surprising there are more women in Al-Anon than men. However, even though 34 percent of A.A. members are women, nothing like a third of Al-Anon members are male. Somehow we are not surprised because, in our society as a whole, women not only tend to offer more support than men, and women tend to see themselves as victims more often as well.

CODA reflects the notion that women are more dependent than men, even though studies indicate women fare better emotionally (not financially!) after a divorce or the death of their husband.

The preponderance of women in OA mirrors our society's view that women are supposed to be slim and trim. On the other hand, extra weight in men, although recognized as unhealthy, is not considered terribly unattractive.

When it comes to adults who grew up in an alcoholic family (Adult Children of Alcoholics), again we find more women than men – in spite of the fact there are more men in A.A. Society strikes again, for it is still more acceptable for women to seek help for emotional problems than it is for men to seek the same kind of help.

The reasons for this difference in power are complex, not totally understood, and certainly beyond the scope of this book. What's obvious, however, is that 12 Step groups do reflect the prejudices of our society when it comes to who has power and who doesn't. The myth of perpetual powerlessness subtly and insidiously reinforces discrimination.

Think, for a moment, what might happen if 12 Steppers accepted the empowerment the Program offers by letting go of the myth of perpetual powerlessness.

Perpetual Powerlessness Is *Not* Attractive

Twelve Step groups wisely don't promote themselves. Instead they rely on the Principle of Attraction. This is expressed in the first half of the 11th Tradition:

> Our public relations policy is based on attraction rather than promotion...

Although some 12 Step organizations occasionally do public information spots on television and radio, by and large reputation of their effectiveness has been spread by word of mouth. This includes talk shows, books and stories written by members and non-members. There are also significant numbers of referrals from law enforcement, courts, medical personnel and spiritual organizations.

Unfortunately, the myths of never-ending recovery and perpetual powerlessness have also spread, both within and outside the movement. Neither is attractive. The movement continues to grow – but, as the statistics indicate, the growth is concentrated in the group that already has the most power.

Some Can't Read

Like most in Program, I grew up going to school regularly. It was assumed I would learn to read, and I did. It wasn't until I was in A.A. that I knowingly ran into a adult who couldn't read.

Andy was in his early 20s, as blonde and white as I am and had a delightful southern accent. Several times he had been asked to read Chapter 5 and had refused. Most of us thought he was shy. In fact, several of us urged him to go ahead and conquer his bashfulness.

Finally he was asked once too often, and admitted to the group he didn't know how to read.

We were all stunned and I even heard one person mutter there was no way he could get sober if he couldn't study the *Big Book*. Fortunately someone took him aside and told him about several literacy programs designed for adults.

Several months later I was working with another young women who came out of the ghetto in Denver. She needed a job badly, and had some experience in housekeeping in motels. She told me the best approach was to simply go to several and see if any of them were hiring. Since she didn't have a car, I offered to drive her around.

I waited in the car at the first motel while she went in to talk to the manager. Moments later she came out, looking shaken, holding an application in her hand. I suggested she go ahead and fill it out while we were there, and her face fell even more.

I realized she couldn't read. When I asked her directly, she admitted the truth, with great shame. Because I knew who to ask (white privilege?), I was able to get her a job, but she didn't stay long and I never knew what happened to her.

I do know that these two people taught me volumes about some of the practical aspects of "being disadvantaged."

If You're Already Powerless

When I was 16 years sober I ended up in the Salvation Army shelter in Fort Lauderdale, Florida for about 10 days. I landed there because a boat delivery went wrong and I was stuck with very little cash, knowing no one – I headed for the shelter so I'd have a safe place to sleep and bathe while I got sorted out.

The shelter was on the edge of the black ghetto – literally. The manager was a white male; there were a few more people of color than whites in the dorms. We had to leave the shelter each morning by 7 a.m. and return by 5:30 to be assured a bed. The theory was we could use the daytime hours on the street to look for work. The reality was there wasn't much work in the area and if you didn't have a car, it was almost impossible to find anything because the public transportation system was very poor. There was, however, an A.A. meeting each morning within walking distance of the shelter. I went.

That meeting had more people of color in attendance than I was used to, but we whites were still in the majority. While I attended, whites always led it – usually white men.

One of the contacts I made there took me deep into the ghetto to a recovery meeting offered by a coalition of church groups. The leaders were a black woman and a black man – both ministers. The make-up of the 20 or so attendees was largely people of color, mostly black. I was one of three or four whites.

I was astounded at this meeting! The whole emphasis was on building our self-worth up so we felt we deserved to recover. Since my own self-worth had been hammered because of my situation, I felt my own spirits lift as the ministers led us in a discussion of why we were worthy, why we were good people and why we were worthy of recovery.

Although I had some self-worth problems when I came to Program, it had never occurred to me I didn't deserve to get sober. It also had never occurred to me that other people, like many at this gathering, might feel differently. The notion of getting sober and being able to get a decent job was an almost impossible dream for lots of them, not because they were stupid people, but because of where they lived – in the ghetto.

There were, however, other major differences between most of the people in the group and myself.

First, I'd been sober a long time, and wasn't in danger of drinking – I'd just gotten in some trouble. I knew I would be able to step out of this dilemma with not much trouble, and that's what happened. A (white) lesbian couple took me home for about three days. A few days later a young (white) man said I could stay on his boat and not worry about the rent until I got a job. I got a job and my life went on with another interesting story to tell.

All I had needed was a hand. A place to stay, access to a phone, and I was able to make my way – not because I was super smart or very talented, but because I'm white, had held jobs and generally knew what to do.

The reality for most of the others, however, was much different. It wasn't simple for them to step out of the degradation of the ghetto – their skin color dictated otherwise. They couldn't, for instance, walk into a large hotel and use the phones the way I could. If they tried, they were at least watched closely if not stopped.

They couldn't show up at an interview and automatically expect to be treated well. While an interview process might hold to the letter of anti-discrimination laws, it was obvious that most places preferred a white woman to a black one. The only times this wasn't true were in minimum wage, no-tip jobs. These people were powerless in a way I had never considered powerlessness before.

Drugs and alcohol were pervasive in this ghetto, like most. Drug dealing was *the* most effective way to earn money – there just weren't many choices, even poor ones. Many homes didn't have a phone – they are too expensive. Not having access to a phone makes job hunting extremely difficult – prospective employers have no way to contact you for interviews.

Many couldn't read – even though they had gone to school. Most had never held a job, didn't know how to find one and wouldn't know how to keep one – not because they're lazy or slow, they're not. It's simply because their life experience doesn't prepare them for much but more poverty.

Think about it; if you can't read, you can't find jobs listed in the paper, you can't fill out an application and you can't follow written instructions. You're stuck, really stuck.

Yes, people do get out of the ghetto – we hear those stories. But those who do get out are exceptional people, usually with an exceptional family. Like the rest of society, however, most people in ghettos are average. The truth is the average person in the ghetto has much less chance of getting a job than the average person outside the ghetto.

When someone from this sort of background comes to a 12 Step group and is told they will be perpetually powerless, even if they let their addiction go and work the Steps, they are rightfully horrified. They know they are already powerless, and not just over their addiction. The myth of perpetual powerlessness becomes a message of no hope at all. Is it any surprise most don't stay?

An Integrated Experience

About two years later, long since home, I ended up at Glide Memorial Church (http://www.glide.org/) in San Francisco. This church is in the heart of the Tenderloin, serves some 3,000 meals a day to the homeless and almost homeless there and is a truly integrated church. It's integrated racially, economically and in terms of gender issues.

At the end of the first service I attended, Cecil Williams, the Minister, called up a group of about a dozen mostly black men and introduced them as having completed the men's crack recovery program at the church. Each one of them introduced themselves by their first and *last* name and the congregation went wild with applause and congratulations.

My AA training immediately resisted the use of last names, but it was obvious that what they were doing was working, so I let go of my negative judgment and watched. There was true acknowledgment for their considerable accomplishment. It was also obvious that they had used a 12 Step approach, but omitted the anonymity, along with the myth of powerlessness. There was no doubt that they considered recovery a powerful action. They expected these people to become and stay powerfully recovered.

Slowly I began to understand that it makes no sense to ask people who know powerlessness at a level I'll never understand to adopt an attitude of perpetual powerless in order to recover. It makes even less sense when you recognize perpetual powerlessness is a myth.

The myth of never-ending recovery adds to the myth of perpetual powerlessness. It portrays addiction/dysfunction as hopeless even when it's not practiced. This myth just makes it less likely someone who already feels powerlessness over everyday things will even make the attempt to recover.

Although many overcome the myths, at least in part, and recover from their addiction/dysfunction, many more don't. The myths of perpetual powerlessness and never-ending recovery are an unnecessary barrier for those who experience powerlessness in the daily context of their lives.

The 12 Step Movement Can Change

It's certainly not the 12 Step movement's job to change society, but it can, and should, change itself. Like letting go of an addiction/dysfunction, the change starts with individuals.

As individuals become aware of the myths of perpetual powerlessness and never-ending recovery, as they see how these myths damage both themselves and the fellowships that have saved their lives, they will begin to let these myths go.

When individuals began to claim to be powerfully recovered, the myths will gradually disappear. The movement will become more attractive to those who have shunned it because of the myths. The face of the movement will become more diverse. It will no longer reflect society's prejudice so accurately. The movement will do better – it will begin to mirror our population.

There is so much to gain, both for those already in recovery and for all those who need recovery. How can we possibly lose?

Chapter 8

The Courage To Change

The essence of all growth is a willingness to change for the better and then an unremitting willingness to shoulder whatever responsibility this entails. (p. 115)

It takes courage to change. Often, before we do, we need to discover the fears we have about the changes we want to make. One way to do this is to imagine that the change has already taken place and notice what mental objections or reservations we have to that image. It's not unusual to find that the fears are, at least in part, illusory or false.

Fears About Being Powerfully Recovered

Claiming to be powerfully recovered is, for most of us, a major change. Like other changes, we may discover we're blocked or fearful.

In general, the fears tend to fall in the following categories. You may discover that some of these fears fit you.

Fear Of A Slip

We've discussed fear of slipping and seen how the Program assures us it's an unwarranted fear if, and it's a big if, we work the Steps. In addition, however, it should be pointed out that sometimes others in Program will try to frighten people about slips. This can be particularly true when someone seems to be flying in the face of conventional thinking.

If this should happen to you, your best course is to stay calm and don't fight. Look carefully within to see if anything that's being said is true for you. If it is, deal with it through the Steps; if not, relax and trust.

Honest Mistake

When I had been sober a little over three years, someone with more than 20 years asked several of us what we would do if we somehow had a drink by mistake. He suggested that it might happen at a party, and pointed out that, if we were truly successful with the Program, we would be out and about in the world.

I felt an immediate fear in my gut, but thought about the parties I had attended in the past, and those I might attend in the future. I actually formed a picture in my mind of picking up what I thought was a 7-Up, taking a swallow and discovering it was actually gin and tonic.

I thought about it some more and realized that for me the key would be in what I did next.

"If it were an honest mistake," I said, "I'd put the glass down and not worry about it much – oh I'd probably say a prayer or too and make sure I talked with someone about it before long, but it wouldn't be a problem. If, on the other hand, I took another swallow, I hope I'd have the honestly to admit I'd had a slip."

Years later something like this actually happened. I had a couple of rough moments before I realized it wasn't a slip. I was glad someone had thought to ask me about it long before.

Fear Of Loss Of Community

For many of us, the Fellowship has been a homecoming. Our group(s) feels like family. We are afraid if we disagree we will lose the community that has become so important to us. It can happen. Groups caught up in 'group-think' can be unforgiving.

If you find yourself in this position, it may be time to begin exploring other groups in your area. Chances are, you'll find one or two that are more open-minded.

Don't overlook the possibilities of finding community in groups outside the 12 Step movement as well. As you grow in recovery, you'll probably find yourself wanting to stretch your wings and explore.

Remember, you don't have to leave your group all at once, although you may find yourself more comfortable talking a bit less about becoming powerfully recovered. It can take some time to find a new community, inside or outside the 12 Step movement.

Go easy with yourself.

Fear Of Taking Personal Responsibility

Accepting personal responsibility is part of what the Program is all about. We discover, as we work the Steps, that we can no longer use others to blame for our addiction/dysfunction on others. Personal responsibility, of course, goes beyond this, and sometimes we want to avoid it.

Often the fear is that we will have to act on some of our dreams. We may find we need to take some risks, to stretch and find out what we really can do.

The myths of perpetual powerlessness and never-ending recovery keep us from growing to our full capacity. Part of that capacity is being responsible for all our actions, attitudes and thoughts. Claiming to be powerfully recovered means, among, other things, we can no longer our addiction/dysfunction as an excuse for our attitudes and behavior. This can be a scary idea, but once we let it go we find more freedom, grace, and balance.

The Serenity Prayer

The Serenity Prayer sums up much of the 12 Step Program. It acts both as a way to keep us in the present moment and a belief about what can happen in the future. It reads:

> God, grant me the serenity to accept the
> things I cannot change, the courage to
> change the things I can, and the wisdom
> to know the difference.

This prayer so pervasive and powerful, it deserves a detailed look.

Serenity And Acceptance

Serenity – the very word conjures up of mental pictures of calm and unruffled repose. When we first come to Program, calm seems an impossible dream, but as we work the Steps we discover it is indeed possible. We gradually come to experience fewer internal storms and the chaos we've created in our lives begins to get sorted out.

In fact, sometimes we begin to worry that we'll have too much serenity and end up bored – but this rarely turns out to be a real problem – at least not for any length of time.

Of course, none of this is possible without acceptance. Acceptance, it turns out, involves much more than the acceptance of our addiction/dysfunction. We find we need to accept many more things in life, the good, the bad and the indifferent.

This is far from easy! We long for control, even when we know it's not possible. Usually, we come to acceptance after at least a bit of a struggle.

Fortunately, with practice, we discover acceptance is simple. It becomes familiar, even if it never becomes easy.

The Things We Cannot Change...

The most obvious thing we cannot change is, of course, our addiction/dysfunction which is as much a part of us as the color of our hair and eyes. The 12 Steps do, however, give us the opportunity to change how we respond to the fact of our addiction/dysfunction. And it is in this change that we may become powerfully recovered.

Another major thing we cannot change is other people. When we were practicing our addiction/dysfunction, we were often convinced that 'if only' someone else would change we'd be just fine. It doesn't work that way. We only have the ability to change ourselves.

The Things We Can ...

Fortunately there are many things we can change, for change is what the Program is all about. It is about changing ourselves.

What we fail to recognize is what happens around us when we change ourselves. We truly have more influence than we recognize. When we change, we seem to open up a space for others to change as well. It doesn't always happen the way we want, but we can't overlook the possibility.

Of course, we can't change ourselves with the hidden agenda that someone else will change. It doesn't work. We find we really haven't changed and we may have created bigger problems than we started with.

We need acceptance, honesty and humility about the changes we make. We need to be sure we're not locked into expectations.

When these elements are in place, our changes will have a large impact on us, and perhaps on others.

The Wisdom...

Wisdom is an interesting word. It, of course, comes from the word, wise, which is related to an Old English word, *witan,* meaning 'to know.' It's my experience that wisdom really has two sources – those things that we learn, and those ideas, intuitions, knowing, that we have within.

There are almost unlimited resources for learning, both in a formal and in an informal way. In Program we learn from each other, from approved and unapproved literature, from the experiences shared by others, and from our own experience.

The intuition, ideas, and knowings we have within can be more difficult to access, but are of at least equal importance. The inventory Steps help us clear away many of the old ideas that can interfere with that 'still small voice.'

The 11th Step,[28] with its suggestion about meditation, gives us a way to begin to listen and hear the inner voice. But notice, the 11th Step also suggests we ask for the *power* to carry out the knowledge we gain working the Step.

Part of wisdom is, I believe, recognizing and accepting that we do have the ability to act – we do have power. To deny this, to insist on saying we are perpetually powerless is to deny a major part of the program.

---

[28] Step 11 is: Sought through prayer and meditation to improve our conscious contact with God *as we understood God,* praying only for knowledge of God's will for us and the power to carry that out.

A Final Story - The Secret

A story is told[29] about a young person who decided the only way to be happy was to have a problem-free life. At first, this youth thought (as young people often do) that simply wishing would make it so, but that didn't work. No matter how many wishes were wished, this very human being still had problems.

So, being creative, resourceful and curious (like all of us), this person bought and read and worked at using the information in all manner of self-help books, and listened to all kinds of self-help tapes, and watched every self-help video to be found – from the most mundane to the most esoteric. After several years of effort, while it can be said that this person's viewpoint changed a bit, the problems had not gone away!

Deciding that working alone wasn't getting results, our friend began studying with teachers around the world, learning an amazing variety of ways to pray, to meditate, to move while praying, to meditate while moving, to visualize, to say mantras, to hum in a special way, and even more.

But no matter how many prayers were prayed, or hours spent sitting, or days spent fasting, no matter how many chants were sung or mantras said, the seeker couldn't help but notice life still presented problems.

---

[29] The first time I heard this story, which I have modified, Dr. John Gray, author of Men are From Mars; Women Are From Venus, a truly empowering book published by Harper Collins, told it.

It goes, almost without saying, that along the way, much was learned, like how to be helpful and when not to offer assistance, and just how to take responsibility without feeling guilt or too much pride, and how to set goals but not get stuck on expectations, and . . .well, it's hard to recount how much was learned.

But no matter what, problems kept popping up.

As fate would have it, one day quite by seeming accident, our friend met a very old woman. At least, sometimes, she seemed very old – other times it was quite hard to tell if she was old or not.

It was, however, obvious, just by looking at her, that this woman was indeed happy. People felt good just being in her presence. It was whispered among those who gathered around her that the wrinkles in her face, and the whiteness of her hair indicated that she had acquired some wisdom along the way.

This old woman lived in a small house, surrounded by a lovely garden full of flowers and wonderful vegetables, which she tended every day, often humming with contentment. She seemed perfectly happy to have the seeker join her in the garden from time-to-time.

Finally, our friend risked telling her . . .

"I've done so much," our friend said, "seeking happiness, but it all seems for naught."

"How so?" the old woman asked.

"Well, I'm embarrassed to admit it, but in spite of all I've done – all the searching, all the learning, all the practicing, I still have problems."

"Mmmmmmm," she said, "tell me more."

And in rather vivid detail the tale was told – the story of the seeking and the story of the never-ending problems. Eventually the story was over and for a long time they sat together in to cool of the garden.

At last the old woman spoke. "There is a secret you've apparently missed," she said a bit tentatively.

The seeker, by now no longer a youth, certain this woman held the key to happiness sat very still, afraid to say anything at all.

After pulling a few more weeds, she began. "You see," she said, "Each and everyone of us comes in this world with a total of 43 problems. As time passes, and we grow in wisdom, our problems change, but we still and always will have 43 problems – that's just the way it is."

Our very human seeker was aghast. "Can it be that I cannot become truly enlightened? Am I condemned to have 43 problems forever?"

"Well, not quite," the old woman admitted. "There is one problem you can get rid of entirely. If you are successful in ridding yourself of this one problem, your life will change for the better, and all else will fall into place. Go home and think about what I have said," she continued. "You have it within yourself to find the answer. If, by this time next week you haven't figured it out, come back and we'll talk some more."

In great frustration our friend rushed home and double-checked all the self-help books that were stacked in his room, our seeker re-read all the notes, listened to all the tapes, and even prayed for the answer, but no answer came.

At last the week passed and our seeker returned to the old woman's garden, exhausted from all the re-studying. "Please, please," our friend begged. "Tell me about this problem I can get rid of."

She saw that he was truly seeking an answer, and began:

"My friend, we all come into this world with 43 problems and there is only one problem we can ever rid ourselves of entirely. That problem is, in fact, the 43rd problem – and it's one we usually don't even see as a problem."

She paused and our seeker thought she would take forever to continue.

Eventually she began again. "The 43rd problem – the only one you can ever rid yourself of, is the problem of believing that having problems is a problem."

Appendix 1 - What About Anonymity?

Anonymity seems synonymous with 12 Step programs. Most use the word, "anonymous," in the name of their organization, and all of them have picked up A.A.'s 12 Traditions. The 12 Traditions are, in effect, the by-laws of the various groups, and are an important part of what being a 12 Step group is all about.

It is in the Traditions that the prohibition against members using their full names when speaking of their membership in public is formalized. Tradition Eleven states:

> Our public relations policy is based on attraction rather than promotion; we need always maintain personal anonymity at the level of press, radio and films.[30]

The 12th Tradition reads:

> Anonymity is the spiritual foundation of all our traditions, ever reminding us to place principles before personalities.

At first glance, anonymity seems to be the focus of each of these Traditions. Closer examination, however, reveals

---

[30] Some of the newer groups add television to this list.

they each address important issues that are not at all dependent on anonymity.

While there was good reason for the emphasis on anonymity when Traditions 11 and 12 were written, those reasons have largely disappeared. There is no longer any need to insist that members of the 12 Step groups hide their identity. The fundamental purposes of the 11th and 12th Traditions can be met without demanding members conceal their membership in public forums. In fact, continuing to require anonymity actually does more harm than good.

Generally, today's 12 Steppers believe that the anonymity requirement was a protection against moral stigma associated with drunkenness. Yet, according to the Foreword of the First Edition of the *Big Book*, the need for anonymity was:

> ...because we are too few, at present to handle the overwhelming number of personal appeals which may result from this publication.[31]

There were just not enough recovered drunks in the beginning to handle the anticipated pleas for help and staying anonymous was a protection against too many calls for help.

But note the phrase, *we are too few, at present . . .* The implication is clear. When the *Big Book* was written, a time was foreseen when the need for concealing A.A. membership would no longer be necessary. The fledgling organization anticipated that, eventually, there would be enough members to allow them to meet the needs of all alcoholics who wanted to get sober. At that point, we can infer, the necessity for anonymity would no longer exist.

---

[31] *A.A.*, p xiii

Rarely Challenged

The reason anonymity is rarely challenged is because, in the past, it has served the 12 Step movement well.

During A.A.'s formative years, there had been much internal struggle. Although the 12th Step contains the purpose of any 12 Step group – to carry the 12 Step message – as A.A. groups sprang up around the country, there was controversy. Questions like who, exactly, should be in charge, and how membership should be determined, and how the message of recovery should be spread were debated with vigor.

Some felt a great deal of centralized control was needed. Others wanted no control or organization at all. Complicated methods of determining who qualified for membership were proposed, only to be shot down by others as too restrictive. Elaborate systems of A.A. hospitals were proposed, both as a way to help others and as moneymaking ventures. None of them came to fruition. Would-be dictators sprung up, sure they knew just how A.A. should grow and promote itself. Some got drunk as a result of their power-driven efforts; others found their groups wouldn't put up with such attitudes and calmed down.

These controversies demonstrated how the young society could get into serious trouble. The Traditions were worked out to prevent such problems from reoccurring.

The 11th Tradition

A.A. took some time to become well known. Gradually, the press began to get curious and as articles about the young organization and its accomplishments were published in popular magazines, the real growth of Alcoholics Anonymous began. Although this interest was welcome, it was also feared that all the publicity would lead to individual bids for power causing all sorts of problems.

This fear was not without foundation. One of the founders, Bill W., had a long history of being a real promoter, and such a disposition was certainly not unique.

By the time the Traditions were written, there had been an attempt by a liquor company to get either A.A. or individual A.A. members to endorse their promotion of moderate alcohol use. At least one member was tempted, but was talked out of it by his group.

Several groups had almost collapsed under self-appointed dictators who were sure they had the right answers for everyone. And a grandiose plan for building large A.A.-sponsored, moneymaking hospitals and recovery centers, complete with A.A. members heading them up (and using their membership in A.A. as their authority), had not only resulted in failure, but in several of the proposed directors getting drunk. It was becoming apparent that when the spotlight of publicity was turned on an individual, the individual was at risk.

There was also concern that those in the spotlight would appear to speak for A.A. as a whole, when in fact, they didn't. It was also feared that if a well-known A.A. member got drunk, the organization's image would be tarnished.

So the concept of anonymity was honed. Although members were encouraged, for example, to speak to interested civic groups about A.A., they were to do so without using their last names. The press was requested to write stories about A.A. without using the last names of members. Personal publicity was to be shunned.

Although initially unrecognized, it was soon realized that the requirement for anonymity at the public level, put, for the most part, an effective stop to the drive for power. The result not only protected the organization, but seemed to help enforce a valuable humility for individual members as well – at least those who tended to want publicity. In the early days of recovery, it was assumed that most, if not all alcoholics suffered from an excess of pride. Thus humility, as the spiritual component of the 11th and 12th Tradition, was born.

Changing Times

Today, many of the problems that triggered the anonymity requirement have changed – not only for alcoholics, but for the 12 Step movement as a whole.

One of the biggest shifts has been the recognition that not all addicts seek power over others. In fact, it's safe to say that more actually suffer from lack of self-worth. We'll speak more of this later.

Of course, another major shift has been the recognition that addiction/dysfunction is a disease and not a moral issue. By and large, particularly when it comes to substance abuse, members no longer need to fear, say, losing jobs if it's discovered they are 12 Step members.

As the 12 Step movement has grown, there have been many anonymity breaks – some by well-known people. These personal revelations have served to attract even more people to recovery. If any of the stars have slipped, there's been little notice of the fact, and it certainly hasn't hurt the movement.

In fact, anonymity breaks have occurred right along with the development of 12 Step groups addressing problems other than alcoholism. Authors with name recognition have written books on recovery, and others have gained recognition with books that have been largely responsible for founding some of the newer 12 Step organizations.

Prominent sports figures, journalists, movie and television stars and even politicians have let it be known directly or indirectly that they participate in one or more 12 Step group.

Less well-known anonymity breaks happen all the time. For example, it's not unusual for corporations to find 12 Step members to lead employee organizations that address addiction/dysfunction. Counselors working with these issues are often in recovery themselves, and many are quite public about their membership.

The 12th Tradition

The major purpose of all the Traditions is to create unity among the groups without forcing them to be identical in the way they function. The controversies of the early years made it clear that such a set of guidelines was needed. Many of the original conflicts centered around the strong and differing opinions of individual members. There was real fear that those with the most charisma would be able to sway a decision. Thus the emphasis on:

...principles before personalities.

Before long it was also recognized that requiring anonymity went a long way toward curbing the dangers of personality cults and nudging the would-be stars toward some humility. That is the central purpose of the 12th Tradition – the reminder that personalities should be set aside when considering issues that affect 12 Step members, groups and organizations. In other words, members are (or should be) motivated by the higher purpose of the good of the group instead of any personal gain.

Obviously, *principles before personalities* is a grand idea, both inside and outside the 12 Step movement. However, the question today is, does this worthy goal require anonymity?

The answer is no!

It's true that the 12 Step member who is, or becomes, famous will have a different set of problems to deal with the one who is less well known. Celebrity, or the lack of it, however, has little if anything to do with an individual placing principles before personalities.

Further, the fear that any one person can harm the movement is no longer realistic. There are just too many people involved for a personality cult to do any real damage

What's Really Going On?

Of course, not many 12 Steppers have the opportunity to go public with their membership. It's a small minority indeed who interest the public in any way at all. The anonymity breaks that have occurred would seem to have done little harm, and even some major good.

Yet each 12 Step group continues to insist on paying lip service to the anonymity portions of Traditions 11 and 12. What's really going on with the continued insistence on anonymity?

Public acknowledgment, or at least its possibility, seems natural, supportive and helpful to others.

In most cases, the member's destructive behavior was quite well known before they came to recovery. Even members of groups dealing with less obvious problems tell how, after they work the program, they realize they were unsuccessful in hiding their addiction/dysfunction.

There are several problems caused, or reinforced by the requirement for anonymity. They include shame, promotion of secrecy, the prolonging of guilt, all of which puts limits on self-worth.

Shame And Loss Of Control

In any addiction/dysfunctional behavior, loss of control is a major issue. After all, if alcoholics could control their drinking, they wouldn't be alcoholics; if co-dependents could take better care of themselves, there would be no need for CODA, etc. etc. etc.

It doesn't matter what sort of problem the 12 Step group is addressing – there would be no need for the group if the behavior it addresses were controllable or changeable without it.

In order to regain command of their lives, the person trapped in an addiction/dysfunction must first admit to loss of control.

Unfortunately, there is a great deal of shame in admitting that loss of control. Even with the growing understanding of addiction as a disease, it is still seen, in the beginning of recovery, as a personal failure. The shame comes, in part, because as human beings we like to believe we are in control. Our society reinforces the illusion that we should be in control – at least most of the time.

But the truth is, no one has total control over their lives. The constant attempt to control deadens the spirit, not only because the effort is doomed to failure, but because it stifles natural spontaneity. To feel shame for losing control is to feel shame about an important facet of being human. To feel shame because of addiction/dysfunction is to feel humiliation about something that one has no control over at all.

Joining a 12 Step group is the first step in regaining control. Unfortunately, the prohibition about "going public" subtly reinforces the idea we have something to hide.

Receiving acknowledgment for a job well done is important for self-worth. Although 12 Steppers do receive some acknowledgment at meetings and from family and friends, the anonymity requirement prevents them from receiving it in a larger, more public way.

The lack of even potential public acknowledgment also means a lack of public role models for others to follow. Recovery should be celebrated, not hidden.

Anonymity Promotes Secrecy

It's particularly difficult to accept the need for required anonymity because anonymity promotes secrecy. Keeping secrets about the addiction/dysfunctional behavior is one of the symptoms of the problems. Incest survivors kept their abuse hidden while it was happening and often long afterwards; recovered gamblers tell how they snuck around to do their betting. No matter what the problem, chances are sufferers tried to keep it secret.

Many 12 Step groups rightly emphasize the need to keep no secrets at all, and for all of us a major part of our healing comes in letting go of the secrets – first to ourselves and then to others.

The continued insistence on anonymity is a damaging double message.

Anonymity Promotes Guilt

Everyone who comes to a 12 Step recovery program feels at least some guilt about their addiction /dysfunction. Much of this guilt is about the problem itself, and much about the behavior it led to. This guilt is one of the elements that help people seek recovery in the first place.

But there is nothing to be gained by continuing to feel guilty for what's past. Quite the contrary – recovery actually helps us understand that our past can be of use.

Yet the requirement for anonymity leads people to believe they still have something to feel guilty about, even when their recovery has led to massive, positive behavior changes.

In the groups that deal with victims – Incest Survivors Anonymous, ACoA, and the various "Anon" groups that help friends and families like Al-Anon, Nar-Anon, Gam-Anon, etc., requiring anonymity tends to perpetuate the idea that their members are somehow at fault for becoming victims in the first place.

There is a huge difference between taking responsibility and feeling guilty. The former is an act of courage; the latter keeps people feeling like they are less than whole.

Anonymity and Self-Worth

Lack of self-worth is a constant theme in any 12 Step group. We come in feeling wrong and unworthy – and often as if we've lost our identity to our addiction/dysfunction. As we move through the Steps, the layers of emotional trauma are removed. Self-worth is restored, because we rediscover ourselves and the fact that we can act powerfully on our own behalf – without the substance and/or dysfunctional behavior.

A major part of self-worth is the willingness to be seen. That is, true self-acceptance means we are no longer ashamed of who we have been, who we are, and who we are becoming. The requirement for public anonymity puts an effective stop to our growth because it prevents us from fully stepping out onto life's stage.

The Individual's Right To Choose

In spite of my own willingness to break my anonymity, I am far from saying that everyone in a 12 Step group should go public. Rather, I am suggesting that there should be choice.

There is much to be gained by removing the requirement for public anonymity. Those who are in a position to do so will gain from coming out of hiding. Not only that, but their public admission, even celebration, will help remove any remaining stigma, give lie to rumors that 12 Step organizations are somehow secret and closed societies, and will provide real role models for others who want and need help.

Of course, with such choice comes responsibility. That responsibility includes making it clear that we are speaking as individuals, not as representatives of any organization. It also includes the responsibility to respect, and protect, others' right to remain anonymous if they so choose.

The decision to break anonymity at a public level is a highly personal one, not to be taken lightly. People must have assurance that their membership in any 12 Step group will be held in confidence. Knowing one can come anonymously to a 12 Step group and stay anonymous is a vital part of the principal of attraction. When a member does decide to go public, it must be with the understanding that he or she will protect the identification of all other members. But, as the anonymity breaks have shown us, there is really no reason to fear that others will be exposed.

Perhaps the 11th Tradition could be re-worded to make this even more effective. Something like this might work:

> Our public relations policy is based on attraction rather than promotion. We need always protect the anonymity of others, even of we choose to break our own.

This keeps the principle of attraction while allowing individual freedom.

Nor does the removal of the requirement for anonymity remove our obligation to protect the group and our 12 Step organization as a whole. Principals before personalities must be the ultimate goal, along with the rest of the 12 Traditions, for it is the unity of the whole that allows the individual to recovery. A rewording of the 12th Tradition along these lines might be a more honest approach:

> Principles before personalities is the spiritual foundation of all our Traditions.

Removing the requirement for anonymity has no effect on the primary purpose of 12 Step Programs, nor on any of the other, vital 12 Traditions.

Our Need To Make Our Own Choice

We need to be free to make our own choice about anonymity. For freedom is the ultimate goal of all 12 Step programs – freedom from the addiction/dysfunction – freedom to be all we can be in whatever form this takes. We need the freedom to make our own choice about anonymity, not have it imposed.

Removing the anonymity requirements from the 11th and 12th Traditions will allow us to focus more emphatically on the principles and leave the personalities, anonymous or not, truly behind. It would increase our ability to be of service to others, and allow each of us to become all we can be.

Appendix 2 - Some Thoughts About God

A basic tenet of the 12 Step Program is developing a relationship with "a God of our understanding." Fortunately, there is much latitude in this phrase. I've heard at least one person claim to get sober by praying to a light bulb.

There's no denying, however, that in our mostly western culture, the very title "God" tends to conjure up one or another versions of the male Christian God. This may be changing. As globalization increases, there is an amazing mix and match of religions showing in 12 Step organizations. You may find yourself in a group where someone protests the saying of the Lord's Prayer at the closing because it's a Christian prayer. If you listen closely you might hear someone saying 'Blessed be' instead of 'Amen.' Over coffee or tea you might find yourself listening closely trying to understand someone who has faith, but no specific God.

When I first came to Alcoholics Anonymous, the concept of a more or less Christian God was hardly ever questioned – and when it was there really was very little open-mindedness. Today, thankfully, we have many opportunities to explore and define beliefs that work for us.

The Sex of God

Some time in my first couple of years I began to question what I meant by 'a God of my understanding.' I found I really didn't have much of an idea at all. I began to ask that which I called God for more information, even a vision! And I got one, through a dream state.

What I saw was an infinitely large and infinitely beautiful diamond of which I was but one facet. This satisfied me for a while, although I was disappointed to discover it was not original with me, but is considered by some to be an archetype.

In my fifth year, while driving down the freeway I realized I was again thinking about my understanding of God. As I got ready to make a lane change I glanced in the rear view mirror and for some reason saw myself as well as the traffic behind me. The Biblical quote, "So God created him in his own image . . ." Gen. 1:26 KJV came to me and I had one of those 'ah-hah' experiences.

I recognized that I always thought of God as male, which said something rather profound and sad about my own view of myself.

It seemed to me then, and still does today, that if, as a woman, I can't even conceive of a female God or Goddess, I'm denigrating the feminine image – including my own. Always seeing a male God is hardly a place of balance for a woman. So I began to work at perceiving God as female.

Over time I succeeded, at least most of the time. Today I claim the Goddess.

Of course, some have argued with me. Generally, the argument is that the Deity is sexless. That doesn't set well with me, for gender and sexual desire are far too important to assume a genderless God.

What I really believe is that God is truly all – female, male and genders we've never imagined, as well as everything else, known and unknown.

But it was important that I open myself to the possibilities of a female Deity. It was an important part of finding my own power.

Pagans & 12 Stepping

The term, Pagan, can include lots of things – Wicca, the Earth Based Spirituality of the Unitarian Universalist Church, the teachings of Jungian Margot Adler, the ritual of Starhawk, American Indian Traditions – the list grows and grows, and so does the interest of 12 Steppers in spiritual expressions and practices in these areas.

My personal definition of God has changed and grown over time. At this writing it is more pagan or earth based than not. What I mean is, roughly, that the Source of All expresses through everything. I often refer to the Goddess because I need to remind myself (and others) of the feminine side of the sacred.

So how does this work with the Steps? Beautifully, really. The simple approach is just to substitute Source, Goddess (named or unnamed) or whatever suits you when the word, God, is used in the Steps.

For example, Step 3 would become: Made a decision to turn my will and my life over to the Source.

Paganism, in all its forms goes deep. It recognizes that each of us has access to the power of that which we are a part of and which we honor. More specifically, Pagans teach that each one of us has Power deep within ourselves – power to act on our own behalf. It's not exactly individual power, but a Power that is shared and shaped and sustained by All.

At first glance this might seem to be in conflict with the 12 Steps because of the myth of perpetual powerlessness. So often 'round the tables, 12 Steppers say, and seem to believe that the fact that they are powerless over their addiction means they are also powerless over everything else in life. I call this a myth because two things are obvious to me:

Admitting to an addiction and coming to a 12 Step Program is a tremendous act of Power – Power in the best and highest sense of the word.

As we let go of our addiction, our power to act is restored – to claim otherwise is to be stuck in being a victim.

Take a new look at the Steps. See how each one actually empowers you. Listen to the soft, wise voice within. Claim your own Power.

Light the candles and incense, join a circle, beat the drum and ring a bell; cast some cards, or a set of Runes or let a book fall open where it will and read. Create your own ritual anew each day. Look for the Source in everything – everything around you and within you and within your own actions.

Celebrate!

Celebrate the Goddess in you and in all others; celebrate our wonderful beleaguered planet and the universe she rides in. Weave your web. Know that perfection is for the Goddess, and not all your strands will hold, but even in their unraveling are lessons to teach you to weave again, more surely and with more love.

Blessed Be!

No Deity Or Many

Many spiritual traditions don't embrace the idea of a single Deity. They base their beliefs and practices on a different understanding of the world and universe. For example, Buddhists practice meditation as a way to move toward right living and the cessation of suffering. There is no 'god' in the western understanding of the word. Rather, Buddhism is a way of being. You can find a good description at: http://www.buddhanet.net/mag_bud.htm Taoism is another system that doesn't hold with a single god - http://www.beliefnet.com/index/index_10037.html

On the other hand, there are plenty of spiritual traditions that believe in multiple deities. Hindus have a pantheon of Gods and Goddesses (http://www.beliefnet.com/index/index_10003.html); so do many of the earth-based practices.

The point is, of course, that there are many ways to think about the 'God' question, and probably almost as many beliefs to go with that thinking. The 12 Step Programs, with their phrase 'God of our understanding' opens the door for anyone, no matter what their beliefs are.

Gender-Neutral Chapter 5

Many 12 Step meetings open with a reading of a portion of Chapter 5 from the *Big Book*, which was written in 1935. Back then, it was understood that 'he', 'him,' etc. were meant to include both male and female.

Since then, of course, we've come to recognize the power of language. It's generally accepted that gender-neutral terms are desirable. Here is a portion of Chapter 5 substituting gender-neutral terms.

The first time I heard Chapter 5 read this way at a meeting I was first shocked, and then delighted. I hadn't realized what an effort it had been to mentally translate the words so they truly reflected my gender.

Most of the changes are to the word 'Him' which have been changed to God. While it's true the word 'God' has a masculine flavor in western cultures, it is surely closer to gender-neutral.

How It Works

Rarely have we seen a person fail who has thoroughly followed our path. Those who do not recover are people who cannot or will not completely give themselves to this simple program, usually men and women who are constitutionally incapable of being honest with themselves. There are such unfortunates. They are not at fault; they seem to have been born that way. They are naturally incapable of grasping and developing a manner of living which demands rigorous honesty. Their chances are less than average.

There are those, too, who suffer from grave emotional and mental disorders, but many of them do recover if they have the capacity to be honest.

Our stories disclose in a general way what we used to be like, what happened, and what we are like now. If you have decided you want what we have and are willing to go to any length to get it -- then you are ready to take certain steps.

At some of these we balked. We thought we could find an easier, softer way. But we could not. With all the earnestness at our command, we beg of you to be fearless and thorough from the very start. Some of us have tried to hold on to our old ideas and the result was nil until we let go absolutely.

Remember that we deal with alcohol, cunning, baffling, powerful! Without help it is too much for us. But there is One who has all power, that One is God. May you find God now!

Half measures availed us nothing. We stood at the turning point. We asked God's protection and care with complete abandon.

Here are the steps we took, which are suggested as a program of recovery:

1. We admitted we were powerless over alcohol, that our lives had become unmanageable.

2. Came to believe that a Power greater than ourselves could restore us to sanity.

3. Made a decision to turn our will and our lives over to the care of God *as we understood God.*

4. Made a searching and fearless moral inventory of ourselves.

5. Admitted to God, to ourselves, and to another human being the exact nature of our wrongs.

6. Were entirely ready to have God remove all these defects of character.

7. Humbly asked God to remove our shortcomings.

8. Made a list of all persons we had harmed, and became willing to make amends to them all.

9. Made direct amends to such people wherever possible, except when to do so would injure them or others.

10. Continued to take personal inventory and when we were wrong promptly admitted it.

11. Sought through prayer and meditation to improve our conscious contact with God *as we understood God*, praying only for knowledge of God's will for us and the power to carry that out.

12. Having had a spiritual awakening as the result of these steps, we tried to carry this message to alcoholics, and to practice these principles in all our affairs.

Many of us exclaimed, "What an order! I can't go through with it." Do not be discouraged. No one among us has been able to maintain anything like perfect adherence to these principles. We are not saints. The point is, that we are willing to grow along spiritual lines. The principles we have set down are guides to progress. We claim spiritual progress rather than spiritual perfection.

Our description of the alcoholic, the chapter to the agnostic, and our personal adventure before and after make clear three pertinent ideas:

(a) That we were alcoholic and could not manage our own lives.

(b) That probably no human power could have relieved our alcoholism.

(c) That God could and would if God were sought.

Appendix 3 - The Slogans

Twelve Step members toss slogans around with great ease. Meeting halls often display a selection of slogans on the walls. We say them to each other, see them on bumper stickers and use them as sort of a code when we're not sure we're talking to another 12 Stepper.

Like so many things in and around 12 Stepping, the slogans are a mixed blessing. They can serve as a quick and needed reminder. Sometimes, however, the slogans perpetuate the myths by passing along the wrong message. They can even be used to shame people, creating more problems than they're worth.

Not all the slogans are based in Program. This wouldn't be so bad if slogans didn't tend to turn into dogma. But because they are easy to remember, we often use them without thinking. They take on an authority they may not deserve.

Slogans seem to be proliferating! There's a site that, at this writing, lists 252 of the darn things:
http://www.geocities.com/HotSprings/Spa/2973/index11.html
The following selection is obviously not definitive. I've chosen the ones that I have a strong feeling about, one way or another.

Keep Coming Back!

Said by the group after meetings, after the off-key 'Happy Birthday' song to someone receiving an anniversary cake, and often by individual 12 Steppers to each other, *Keep*

Coming Back may be the most repeated slogan we have. Frequently the phrase, 'it works!' is added.

Small wonder – for coming back to meetings again and again is a major key to early recovery. Depending on where you live, you're likely to hear recommendations like 30 meetings in 30 days or 90 meetings in 90 days. Tokens are often given at the end of the recommended period to celebrate the massive change in behavior – after all, by the time we get to Program few of us have ever experienced anything like 30 or 90 days of abstaining from our addiction. Returning to meetings day after day helps us in many ways. As Tony Robbins of fire walking fame often says, 'repetition is the mother of mastery.' Consider:

- In most meetings we hear the Steps, and we also hear how other people are doing with their program.
- Meetings are great way to pick up tips, and if we choose, to share our own triumphs and problems. There's camaraderie at meetings and it doesn't take long for a newcomer to become part of the group.
- Meetings also offer a substitute activity – if we're used to going to a bar or a street corner or hiding in our bedroom - meetings provide a healthier alternative.
- With little difficulty we make new friends when we attend meetings regularly, replacing the people we spent time with when practicing our addiction.
- When we speak at meetings, we are affirming that we too have an addiction – the *I am a (name your addiction)* is a powerful statement that can lead to positive change.
- Meetings, and the coffee klatches afterward can be fun – and fun has often been missing from our lives.

How long we should keep coming back is a different issue. Unfortunately, the ubiquitous use of *keep coming back* can muddy the matter a bit. Some would have us believe we have to go to meetings for the rest of our lives. This is part of the myth of never-ending recovery, and ignores the fact that, with the 12 Steps, we can become recovered. Recovered, of course, doesn't mean cured – abstaining is a life-long necessity.

Going to meetings forever, however, is not required to stay recovered. The Program makes it clear that, if we work the Steps, we'll be 'granted a new freedom' and be able to re-enter the world as a full citizen.

So *keep coming back* as long as you need and want to – as long as it takes you to work all 12 Steps and until you're sure you don't have to. And always be willing to go to a meeting should your addiction begin to raise its ugly head again.

Knowing ourselves and our vulnerabilities, and being willing to come back, is part of a powerful recovery.

First Things First

This one makes a lot of sense to me, and not just in a 12 Step context. Of course, in the 12 Step framework, this is most often used to remind us to stay away from our addiction/dysfunction.

I think, however, this slogan can generate a recognition about the Steps as well. The order of the Steps fascinates me. Each one builds so neatly on the one before it, yet the focus is always moving forward. I've been known to use this slogan when, for instance, someone is worrying about who they will share their 5th Step with before they've even started their 4th.

Keep It Simple

Doctor Bob actually reminded Bill W. (his Alcoholics Anonymous co-founder) to *keep it simple* when the organization of Alcoholics Anonymous was being formed back in the late 1930s, '40s and early '50s. Dr. Bob's admonition was most likely in response to Bill's well-known propensity for grandiose thinking. It was good advice then and it works well for us today.

The 12 Step Program is actually quite simple – not easy – but simple. It's temping to over-think the Steps, and that over-thinking often becomes an excuse not to do them. You know what I mean. Take, for example, Step Three: Made a decision to turn our will and our lives over to the care of *God as we understood God.*

There's a ton of opportunity to get snarled in intellectualism here, the most likely being trying to define our concept of God. While we may want, at some time, or even several, to really investigate exactly what we might mean by that term, for the purposes of Step Three we don't have to wait for a definition. Instead, we're only asked to decide that we want to, and intend to live our lives on some spiritual basis.

It's a decision, a goal – and we don't need all the answers before we take this step. In fact, at this point in our Program we won't know exactly what that means. It's the willingness that counts here; being willing is keeping it simple.

The same thing is true about doing an inventory – again, not an easy step, but a simple one. We simply need to write down the wrongs we've done – the ones we're aware of at the moment. We don't need a whole life history or lots of delving into the psychological reasons for this or that. All you really need is the list – which is truly keeping it simple.

Unfortunately, some in the Fellowship seem to think the slogan means we shouldn't think at all or use our intellect and intelligence – far from it. We've got a brain and a mind and are meant to use it.

There is, however, a huge difference between thinking clearly and thinking in convoluted circles about essentially unanswerable questions. When we're new to Program our thinking is unlikely to be truly clear – that will come with practice and time.

Some corrupt the slogan by adding to it so it becomes *Keep It Simple Stupid*. This allows the acronym, KISS. I don't think the acronym is worth it. We are not stupid people, not by a long shot and when one person says this to another it's a put-down that adds nothing – in fact it diminishes both the person saying it and the person it's said to.

Keep it simple on your journey to being Powerfully Recovered!

Easy Does It

Easy Does It is seen on walls of 12 Step meeting halls. Sponsors tell their Sponsees, 'easy does it,' and 12 Steppers say it to each other often. Usually it's good advice. Those of us recovering from addictions seem subject to more 'mind storms' than the rest of the world. We can get caught in such mental snarls! *Easy does it!* is often a good solution to what some refer to as 'monkey mind,' particularly if we add a couple of deep breaths!

One of the best uses for *Easy does it!* is to quiet the demand for instant perfection, whether that demand is for our Program or our family, our work and income or any other area in our lives.

When we come to Program we have lots of work to do, and trying to get everything done all at once, and perfectly, is a sure path toward failure. Our first job is our addiction, and for 12 Steppers that means our first job is working the Steps.

Working the Steps is where the addition to *Easy Does It* really makes sense: *But Do It*!

For reasons that I believe have more to do with unfounded fear than anything else, there is an attitude among some in 12 Step Recovery that we have 'to be ready' to work the Steps, particularly the 4th Step. It appears to be a fear that a newcomer will go into some sort of overwhelm and maybe slip because the 4th Step is too hard to handle in the beginning.

What's ignored is that there is *no* indication in the literature that we should take our time – *absolutely none*. In fact, if you read Dr. Bob's story, in the book *Alcoholics Anonymous*, it becomes clear he worked the then Six Steps in an afternoon and evening! (The original six steps contain *all* of the now 12 – they were broken up to provide more manageable chunks). The founders and old timers knew it was imperative that the addict had to take massive personal action to effect the needed changes. The Steps, including Step 4 are a solid plan for taking the action necessary to recover.

I'm not saying everyone must work all the Steps in an afternoon and evening – I didn't, but I was lucky when some member told me I wasn't 'ready' to do the 4th. My sponsor simply snorted and suggested I get on with it and I did, just before my 90th day.

In my opinion, there is no such thing as 'being ready.' Think about it. What would 'being ready' look like? How are you supposed to know if you're there or not? There are no criteria or evidence. Besides, delaying now only makes it easier to delay tomorrow, and tomorrow until we've justified not doing it at all!

Getting down to the work, work on the Steps, is the real solution, and the way to become Powerfully Recovered!

One Day At A Time

I imagine that this is the very first slogan that found its way into the original AA meetings. Can't you just picture a frantic newcomer talking about how difficult he (and yes, it *was* only men in the beginning – and the men didn't think women could be *real* alcoholics, which is another story…) was finding sobriety? I can almost imagine the conversation:

Newcomer: What am I going to do? Next
week I have to go to the office Christmas
party – how will I ever stay sober there!

Oldtimer: (who has a week or less): Slow
down, it's not next week yet. Take it One
Day at a Time!

And a slogan is born – because it's got some real wisdom in
it. For in truth, each one of us has only one day at a time – or
one hour or one moment.

In the first few rocky days of recovery, just abstaining
for that moment, hour, and so on, is truly all we can do. If we
can't do that, there's no point in worrying about tomorrow, or
next week, or whenever.

The *One Day at a Time* philosophy has benefits far
beyond the early days in recovery. It can keep us grounded
in the present – that Holy Instant that is so easy to miss in a
busy and productive life.

Unfortunately, some in 12 Step Groups have taken the
philosophy to mean we shouldn't plan. This is patently false.
A major promise of the Program is to *restore us to sanity*,
and that includes the very human blessing and curse –
planning. We need to set goals, to make appointments, to
design our lives.

Planning doesn't mean we have to leave *One Day at a
Time* behind – the trick is to watch for expectations. It's one
thing to plan and quite another to demand that the plan work
out the way we require it too – in that we have no control at
all. When our plans bring unintended results – and they often
do – all we need do is re-evaluate, accept where we are in
this moment, and start anew.

Knowing, using and accepting the present moment is
part of being Powerfully Recovered!

Let Go And Let God/Goddess

Let go and let God is a favorite slogan. It shows up on
meeting hall walls, on bumper stickers, the sides of mugs
and all sorts of other places. Like so many things in the
Program, this slogan comes in two parts.

Letting go is a major key to being powerfully recovered.
I've always found that my ability to let go is in direct
proportion to my willingness to accept – accept whatever is
going on in my life right now, and without reservation.
I have to come to terms with the issue, whatever it is, much
like I did about my alcoholism/addiction. It wasn't until I
accepted that I couldn't control my drinking that I was able to
let go of attempts at control and go get the help I needed.

With the total and honest acceptance, letting go is
almost automatic. Letting go is a powerful action. It takes
understanding and a certain amount of will, as well as the
willingness to change.

This part of the slogan is meant to be a reminder that
we've turned our lives over to the *care* of a Higher Power.
Properly used, the slogan can put us back in touch with
ourselves as spiritual beings. It can remind us simply to quit
pushing and to breathe, deeply, maybe even more than once.

So often we forget that we have a Higher Power,
however we define that. We think we have to do everything
on our own. Sometimes this is a misguided attempt to stay in
control, to push, to demand that our expectations are met the
way we want them met.

As our world shrinks, this slogan can become a
problem. Not because of what it's trying to teach, but
because it assumes a belief in a single, and usually male
Christian God. But there are lots of belief systems that don't
have a God as we westerners tend to define that. Many
Buddhists and Taoists, for example, concentrate on the right
way of being, not on the concept of a God.

On the other hand, Pagans and Hindus draw from a whole pantheon of Deities – including male and female. *Let go and let God* becomes exclusionary.

Changing the slogan to *Let go and let the God of Our Understanding...* is a bit unwieldy. Maybe it would work better if we changed it to simply, *Let go.*

If You Want To Stay Dry, Stay Out Of Wet Places

Certainly not an official part of Program, this saying has grown up in the Fellowship of Alcoholics Anonymous. I'm always amused that, at least in the United States, we associate 'wet places' with bars – this is probably a holdover from our Prohibition days when much of the discussion surrounded 'wet and dry' as code words for alcohol and alcohol-free. Staying out of bars and away from parties where the emphasis is on liquor is a good idea for AA's, particularly in the beginning. The concept can be translated to other addictions without too much trouble.

A problem with this slogan can arise when it's used either to stop a 12 Step member from going somewhere out of fear, or to lay guilt on someone for going someplace someone thinks might be questionable.

The Program is intended to put us back in the world without fear of a relapse. In other words, after they've worked the Steps, members of Alcoholics Anonymous should be comfortable in bars and parties where liquor is served; Over Eaters Anonymous should be able to go to a holiday party without fear of over eating, etc.

The key is self-honesty. If I, as a recovered alcoholic/addict, want to go to a bar or party for reasonable social or business reasons, I'm fine. If, on the other hand, I'm shaky and want some sort of vicarious thrill, I'm better off not going.

Working the Steps is the surest way for a 12 Stepper to develop the needed self-honesty.

Don't Get Too Hungry, Angry, Lonely Or Tired

HALT is a fairly recent addition to the slogans you'll hear around 12 Step groups. It happens to be one I really like and use for myself a lot, particularly the hungry, angry and tired parts. If I don't eat regularly, my thinking gets really awful. When I was new to Program I actually had to practice eating on a regular basis, and I can still let it slip if I'm too busy.

Anger is one of those emotions that have a bad reputation in 12 Step groups. It often gets confused with resentment. Resentment is actually reliving an anger over and over again. But real, honest and instant anger has its place. After all, it was anger that fueled the civil rights movement in the 1960s and anger that sparked throwing tea in the bay when the colonists didn't like taxation without representation. On a more personal level, anger can signal when we're being treated unfairly or our boundaries are ignored.

It's what we do with anger that counts. When we use it to learn more about ourselves, to set and reinforce boundaries or to right a wrong, we're headed in the right direction. On the other hand, when we let it build to resentment, or use it to lash out inappropriately, we are headed for trouble.

I actually think 'isolated' would be a better term than 'lonely' in this saying, turning it into *Don't get too hungry, angry, isolated or tired.* But HAIT isn't what we're after here, and HALT is. Addicts do tend to isolate, to spend too much time alone. How much is too much is a highly individual question, but moving out to be with people is the antidote. Lunch with a friend, going to a meeting, attending a class – any of these and more can break up the loneliness that can lead to self-pity and self-absorption.

Fatigue can get us into trouble. We don't think well when we're tired, and, as a result, often don't act well. Issues become magnified. Fatigue also affects our health, and I've come to check and see how well I'm doing with my physical well being when I think about this slogan.

If It Ain't Broke, Don't Fix It

There are definitely times when this quaint saying makes sense. It's a good way to avoid perfectionism, which is often a subtle, and unconscious scheme to avoid moving forward. Besides, I'm convinced few of us would recognize perfection even if it walked in the door and introduced itself! I was several years clean and sober before I realized I hesitated trying new things because I couldn't do them perfectly – talk about ego!

Another way this slogan works well is helping people avoid making change just for the sake of change. Not everything needs to be changed; much of who we are is good and true. While we need to be willing for everything to change, the willingness is the key – what's actually needed will flow from there.

Unfortunately, in the Fellowship, this saying is often used to either avoid needed change or as a way to avoid even discussing the possibility of change. This shows up most often when someone suggests a change in meeting format, or suggests we can be powerfully recovered. Sometimes the resistance is subtler with members exhibiting a sense of disapproval of new ideas.

The goal, I think, is not to get bogged down in dogma.

Don't Intellectualize

This one truly drives me nuts. When asked, the people who use it claim to be saying 'keep it simple' in another way. But I don't think so. 'Thinking' is the real issue here, and some would have us believe thinking is a bad thing.

Our ability to think is a gift not to be disparaged. While it's true we may get into mental snarls from time-to-time, someone shouting not to intellectualize rarely helps. There's a huge difference between a mental snarl and actually thinking something through. But mental snarls aren't intellectualizing – they aren't even really thinking – a mental snarl leads nowhere, really.

Thinking, on the other hand, can lead to new ideas, real solutions, insights and personal growth. Thinking can also lead to the recognition that existing ideas, solutions and insights are just fine the way they are.

Sometimes I've been accused of intellectualizing because of my reading. It seems as if some people in 12 Step groups are afraid of new or different ideas.

I don't find anything in the Program that indicates I shouldn't think. Quite the contrary, as a matter of fact – on page 164 of *Alcoholics Anonymous*, the statement is made:

> We realize we know only a little.

How else are we to expand our knowledge if we don't think?

There's a quote from Herbert Spencer at the end of the "Spiritual Experience," the second Appendix of Alcoholics *Anonymous*

> There is a principle which is a bar against all information, which is proof against all arguments and which cannot fail to keep a person in everlasting ignorance – that is the principle of contempt prior to investigation. (A.A. p. 570)

I don't believe it's possible to investigate anything without thinking about it. What do you think?

My Best Thinking Got Me Here

This slogan is, in a way, a corollary of "Don't intellectualize." I suspect the intent is to point out that practicing our addiction demonstrated less than brilliant thinking. While that's certainly true, it's an awfully limited way to look at our thinking.

The slogan is almost always said as a way to demonstrate how poor our thinking is – even after recovery, and I think it's a big mistake. Why thinking should get such a bad name in 12 Step groups is beyond me.

First of all, it was my best thinking that got me to Program – even in the drunken, drugged state I was in. Sure, it was grace, but it was my mind, my thinking that allowed me to accept it. After I'd dried out a bit, it was my thinking that kept me coming back and working the Steps.

Thinking, good, solid thinking, led me to change careers, do a good job with my children, improve my education – the list goes on and on. When I look around me at those in recovery I see some of the finest thinking imaginable. People are taking positive action on their own behalf, going back to school, starting businesses, and reaching out to help others. Every bit of it requires pretty darn good thinking.

This is a slogan I not only don't use, but also will challenge when it's said in my hearing.

Think, Think, Think

Apparently I'm not the only one who favors thinking. This admonition shows up fairly often, and I'm grateful. I truly believe thinking is a good thing, and encourage it wherever and whenever I find it.

Keep The Memory Green

I first heard this after I'd been sober awhile; it's probably a fairly recent addition, and I'm not sure it's a good one, at least over the long haul.

While it's true in the beginning, remembering the horrors I created with my addictions and dysfunctions helped keep me clean and sober, in truth many of those memories have faded. I no longer remember the lurid details, and I don't think I need to.

At some point we have to let go of the past and quit wallowing in what we've done. Our 4th, 5th and 10th Steps make it possible to do just that, face our past and let it go.

To be sure, when I try, I can remember details, but it's an effort now. Does this make me more vulnerable to a slip? Apparently not. I can still talk congruently with newcomers; when I see a drunk or a practicing drug addict I not only recognize the problems, I also feel the genuine compassion that comes from having walked in their shoes. But I don't spend much time thinking about my drinking and using these days.

What is still very clear and 'green' for me, when I happen to think about it, is the sense of emptiness and loss I experienced when practicing my addictions. That barrenness is my 'green' memory now. For me, at least, it seems even more effective than wallowing in the details.

Appendix 4 - We Are Not Powerless Over Our Emotions!

By narcosis[32]

Most people, in and out of the Program, believe that humans are powerless over their emotions. However, I now know this sense of powerlessness is one of life's great misconceptions. While we are relatively (not completely) powerless over emotions from showing up in our lives, we have a huge amount of power about how we respond to, manage and organise our feelings.

If we are doing all the spiritual work we can, and still not feeling great, then perhaps it's time to add to our Stepwork some tips and techniques for emotional recovery as well. If we feel good, we are less likely to be sucked back into active addiction.

---

[32] Anne's Note: Narcosis and I met through the magic of the 'net, and even though we live on almost opposite sides of the planet, (he is from Australia which explains the Australian spelling) have found we have much in common. Through an odd set of circumstances, I had a chance to observe him counsel someone by email. I am impressed with the information he has about emotions. Narcosis gracefully agreed to write the following essay. His email is: narcosis@go.to
His website is: http://go.to/narcosis
32

I wanted to kill myself

I am a recovering addict, and like most addicts, I want feelgoods, and I want them *now!* At this writing, I have been in recovery for 2 years and 7 months, after 25 years of daily-use poly-addiction/alcoholism. As a heroin addict, I felt so badly that I made preparations to kill myself. By a remarkable chain of events, I survived.

In my first year of recovery I felt appallingly bad and in excruciating emotional pain virtually all the time.

In the past year I have felt ecstasy and many other pleasant feelings at least once every day. I feel 90 percent good 90 percent of the time. I don't ask for much more than that. How have I achieved this turnaround? Do I possess a secret formula?

No, I have simply learned a few techniques, and put them into practice. I am building my own feelgood technology[33] and you can too with these and other tools.

Illusions and misconceptions

I am a committed member of Narcotics Anonymous. The 'Anonymous' groups are excellent programs for letting go of addictions. They are spiritually based programs, but do not claim to be emotional programs. Words like 'emotions' and 'feelings' are not in the Steps or Traditions. The emphasis is on a tripartite disease, 'mental, physical and spiritual'. While

---

[33] I have drawn on numerous influences, but wish especially to acknowledge the Program of Narcotics Anonymous, and many principles and techniques taught by Anthony Robbins, the well-known speaker and writer.

It was my good friend Pete Walker (author of *The Tao of Fully Feeling*, Azure Coyote Publishing, 1995) who, 1981, initiated me into the realm of emotional management, and to him I owe the greatest debt of gratitude.

many also achieve serenity, many others continue to experience major emotional upheavals

So perhaps it's a good idea to find tools that can be used for our *emotional* health that complement spiritual practice – techniques that do not conflict in any way with the 12 Steps and12 Traditions.

The Illusion Of External Emotions

First, however, we need to become aware of, and deconstruct, some illusions - illusions that we, as humans, all live with most of the time.

For example, one illusion we all share is that the earth is flat, although photographs from space prove otherwise. Even though we know in our heads that the world is round, we behave and think as if it were flat.

We also think that matter is solid, though it is mostly empty space. We behave and talk as if the sun revolves around the earth – we say it rises and sets. We act as if the days are grouped naturally into weeks of seven days, and believe that the past is actually impinging on our enjoyment of the present.

Similarly, most of us believe that the source or cause of our emotions often comes from outside our bodies. What's seems to me to be true, however, is that everything we think and feel takes place *within* our own bodies, our own 'capsule of meat' as I call it.

By and large, people don't physically affect each other's emotions or thoughts. Yet we habitually imagine that people can influence our feelings and our minds by their words, actions or even thoughts. the children's rhyme is more accurate: "Sticks and stones may break my bones, but names can never hurt me!" Although it feels as if what we are feeling comes from the outside, in truth, what we're feeling is actually our own, internal response to stimuli. As a general rule, we affect only ourselves, and others affect only themselves.

The illusions, however, are strong. We even have expressions that perpetuate them, like:

- "Sandra hurt my feelings."
- "John makes me feel young again."
- "The Rolling Stones turn me on."
- "Winning the lottery made Laura happy."
- "Jack bores me."

In fact, all of the emotions referred to in these examples are entirely generated by us within our own *meat* – our nervous system (especially the brain), our endocrine system, our lymph system – the whole miraculous complex of compound chemicals we call the body.

Fortunately, although the English language has limited emotional symbology, it does contain words and expressions that relate to the bodily presence of our emotions: *gut feeling*; *haven't got the stomach for it*; *spineless*; *hot under the collar*; *tense*; *heartless*, and so on.

Those of us who are in 12 Step programs will no doubt recall the emotional roller coaster of early recovery. Where was this roller coaster taking place? Clearly, it was all in our bodies, not in the air or space.

Once we can internalise, at a deep, 'gut' or 'heart' level, the truth that our emotions are physical phenomena within our personal 'chemistry sets,' we are well on the way to being able to act as our own alchemists and quite quickly become masters of our own emotions.

By the way, it is absolutely essential to separate the *label* we give emotions, from the *feelings* themselves. I ask myself "What am I feeling?" because it is more useful to me than "How am I feeling?" I need to know what I am actually feeling *within* my body as my emotional barometer fluctuates.

The goal is to feel our bodies so precisely, so attentively, that when we have an emotion, we know where and how it is occurring in our bodies. We would do well to cultivate an inner dialog something like this: "It's not up in the sky, so where exactly is this feeling? Is it in my arms, abdomen, upper chest, neck, or a combination of these? Does my face feel warmer and redder? Is there a flow of some chemicals to the top of my shoulders, or do my hands feel somehow different? If so, what part of the hands?" And so on.

Words like 'angry,' 'sad,' 'joyful,' 'reverent,' 'contented' and so on are merely convenient labels. They basically help us *name* our true feelings. Just as a gardener needs to know intimately the plants themselves and not just their names, the answers to our questions about our own emotions are better in terms of sensation rather than labels.

Working backwards

The mind, the body and the emotions are all interlinked and each affects the other. What we do with our minds influences what we do with our bodies, and vice versa. For example, first we decide to paint a picture, then our bodies do it; we pick up a paintbrush, and we start thinking like a painter.

> ## Ways of Processing
>
> **Most Westerners are aware of this:**
> Thinking > Emotions > Bodily behaviour
>
> **Fewer Westerners are aware of this:**
> Bodily behaviour > Emotions > Thinking

What we do with our emotions affects our minds, and vice versa. We feel anxious, and our thoughts become like a swarm of bees (Feelings > thoughts). We think of ourselves as funny, and we start feeling funny (Thoughts > Feelings). What we do with our bodies affects our emotions, and vice versa. We slump our shoulders and faces in a

posture of depression, and we feel depressed (Body >
Feelings). We are feeling bliss and our breathing, heart rate
and posture change to 'bliss' mode (Feelings > Body).

In our Western society, we tend to concentrate on
changing our emotions with our minds. The Freudian model
of therapy set the stage for this a century ago: by talking
about our lives we affect our emotional state. While this is
true, since Freud we have mostly forgotten the fact that we
can change our thinking by first changing our emotions.
Similarly we can get the emotions we want by altering our
bodies.

We often need to work backwards, starting with the
physiology of our bodies, and watching how our emotions
change as a result of changes we make in our physiology.
Then, as our emotions change, our thinking also changes.

In other words, we *can* manage our emotions.
Bearing in mind the importance of the principles of illusion
and working backwards, the list below illustrates some
simple techniques to add to your own. They are a mixture of
techniques that operate on the four levels of our lives: the
physical, mental, spiritual and emotional.

Read them, read them out loud, think about them,
experiment with them – make them your own.

You probably won't use them all at once, at least not
right away. But each one is helpful on its own, and as you
build your collection you'll find yourself experiencing more
and more of the feelings you really want.

Techniques For Emotional Recovery

- This life is not a dress rehearsal. This is my life and I won't mess it up any more.

- The aims of my life are to (a) feel ecstatic and loving; (b) fulfil my dreams; (c) be useful to my family, humanity and the Universe; (d) harm no one and no thing; (e) waste no time. (You, of course, will have your own list.)

- Ninety-five per cent of human suffering is self-inflicted, at least in middle-class Western civilisation. If I can eradicate the 95 percent, I should be able to handle the 5 percent over which I am truly powerless, like stubbed toes, disease, and so on.

- I have suffered long enough and I won't *do it to myself* another day. Time is short. I might die tonight. I lost years to misery. I'd better get serious about my own happiness. If not, I've only got myself to blame.

- I believe in a Higher Power (HP). I commit myself to thinking and behaving as though my life were up to me, in a world that is a mixture of cause-event and randomness, pleasure and pain. My HP assists my thinking and feeling, and will do for me whatever internal changes I can't do for myself.

- I show trust in my own HP by affirming each morning "More will definitely be revealed today. I won't seek, I'll find". Then I wait for the mini-epiphanies and always try to remember to give thanks for them.

- Attitude is everything. I intend to cultivate good attitudes in all things.

- I believe that we reap what we sow. So I try to sow correct thoughts and reprogram bad, useless or unhealthy ones.[34]

- I am predestined for *nothing* and I do *not* have an immutable personality, traits or defects of character.

- I am intrinsically alone. I was born alone and will die alone. I treasure my relationships, and I'm committed to my responsibilities (children and so on) but I try to *feel* and practice my personal aloneness, self-duty and self-preservation. My responsibility to me is making myself feel fantastic and be useful to the Universe while harming no one.

- I am free. I am nobody's servant or whipping boy. I am *not* a victim.

- I want to be at least civil even to my 'enemies'. Even if I haven't in the past.

- Feeling fantastic goes hand in hand with my unfolding understanding of 'spirituality'.

---

34 I imagine thoughts are like segments of cassette tape, and I record over the ones I don't want. Or I picture the useless thought as a weed and pluck it out, planting a new seed in its place. Or I zap old thoughts with a ray gun. You can have great fun with this. It's easiest to do it while meditating. Sometimes I do it quite well. I don't flagellate myself if I fail; I pick myself up off the floor and like a toddler learning to walk, start again. My life begins again from that moment, with new chances and always with choice.

- I 'do' my own feelings. I am not dependent on anyone else. If I have an anxiety attack, I am not attacked by 'anxieties' like a swarm of wasps. I do it to myself. So I refuse to cause any more pain on my body.

- Feelings are like fluids in the body. To control my emotions I must feel *each* feeling in my body.[35].

- Feelings are like muscles. Each one can atrophy, and each can be exercised back to strength. (Not many people know this.)

- Feelings are invoked by (a) body attitude, and (b) mental visualisation. If I can't tap into a present feeling, like 'confidence', at this actual moment, I rummage through my mental filing cabinet and borrow an image from my childhood or a movie I saw or book I read, or a song or piece of music.

- Thoughts follow feelings, probably more than vice versa. If I cultivate the feelings I want, the thoughts *will* follow.

- Feelings follow behaviours. In order to change what I'm feeling, I move my body to imitate and access the feelings I want. I practice in the privacy of my own home, and in the world.[36]

---

35 If I say 'feeling', I mean feeling, not disembodied or ideal, but sensations in the different parts of the body. I don't want to know 'how' I am feeling, I want to know 'what' I am feeling. For example, where in the body, what does it feel like? I try hard not to use labels (angry, hopeful, sad, enthusiastic, etc) disconnected from the actual physical sensation. With practice I improve at my sensibilities.

36 . For example, I can't feel confident if I walk into a room like a loser. I can't feel enthusiastic if I sit slumped and shallow-breathe. To get the feeling we label 'passion', for example, I breathe in, recalling visually a past situation that invokes it. Sometimes I need

- Breathing is as important as body stance. Holding the breath ten times for ten seconds helps me to shift emotions. I try to remember to do it several times a day.

24 Hours Of Feelings

Tomorrow isn't here yet. Christians say: "Take therefore not thought for the morrow: for the morrow shall take thought for the things of itself." (Matt. 6:34 KJV) The Buddha said much the same thing, warning against maya (Hindu: *illusion*). Projecting the future is toxic. I train my head not to travel backwards or forwards in time except for healthy purposes.

There are only 24 hours in the day; every 24-hour period is the canvas with which I work. Every time I tap into 10 seconds of a good feeling is 10 seconds I can't be feeling a bad one. They add up.

I practice 'ODAAT' (One Day at a Time) absolutely rigorously. I try to *make* each day great, not *have* a great day. I take responsibility for the quality of my day and life. The past is *gone* and only 'exists' for experience. Life begins today, right now! What I do, think and feel today will create the matrix for tomorrow's practice.

Make A List

Here's a typical list of feelgood labels. Take a few minutes, read each one aloud with feeling. Notice how your body responds. If you discover you're not getting much body response, stand up and act it out. Watch what happens to your mood.

> Comfort, love, joy, enthusiasm, passion, compassion, sweetness, power, strength, kindliness, peace, serenity, sexiness, awe,

---

to borrow postures from other people and TV characters. This is a good start, and the way I learned as a child.

wonder, adoration, sacredness, divinity,
humour, giggle, belly-laugh, "I'll show
them!", pride, "I'm a winner", "look ma, no
hands", grateful, considerate, confidence,
assurance, popular, conquering hero,
dragonslayer, nurturer, nurtured, mellow,
ecstasy, bliss, 'can do', 'will do', exultation,
'no longer a procrastinator', orgasmic,
favourite poet, favourite
movie/music/song, sunset, sunbaking,
bizarro, wacky, wise, patient, likeable,
trustworthy, good, brave, etc.

Make a list of your own 40 or 50 and feel what each one
does to your body.

Gratitude And Other Feelings

If we work hard on tapping into gratitude, we feel too good
to want to alter our state with mere drugs. Gratitude has an
almost magical ability to lighten and improve our mood.
Starting each morning asking what you are really grateful for
is a powerful way to set the tone of your day.

You'll find that some good feelings are better than
others. Here's an example: to me, 'sexy' feels better than
'sportsmanlike', and 'passionate' feels better than 'neat and
tidy'. But they're all feel-goods – with no withdrawals.
Figure out which feelings you like best and make a habit of
them.

My happiness is NOT dependent on anything or
anyone. Not money, girlfriend, wife, sex, fame, house,
travel. Your's isn't either. Why should we make ourselves
hurt because we haven't got something?

The rituals of being depressed and powerless are far
more difficult than directly tapping into a good feeling.
Nurturing our Top 50 emotions will change our lives by
denying bandwidth/space to the feelings we definitely *do not*
want.

The Brain As Computer

How you talk to yourself determines a great deal of how you feel. That's because your brain is a computer. Ask it sensible, sharpened questions designed to generate creative answers rather than questions that are apt to get answers that will make you feel worse. For example, if you ask yourself (or your oversoul/HP) something like "Why am I so fat/thin/ugly/dumb/unpopular/weak/ etc", your brain is most likely to answer something like: "Because you're a piece of garbage, because you were brought up by morons", and so on!

On the other hand, if you ask "What do I need to do to lose/gain/look good/make friends/get stronger etc." your brain is likely to come up with some truly creative ideas. You can get even better answers if you add a phrase like "and feel ok while I'm doing it."

Then you have to pay attention – usually by writing the better questions down, and writing the answers down as well. Leave the rest to the hyperlink between hand and Web satellite in the sky.

Given a chance, your brain will set to work immediately to answer the questions you put to it. This, I believe, is why Jesus said, "Ask, and it shall be given to you: seek and ye shall find; knock, and it shall be opened for you." (Matt. 7:7 KJV). If you pray, make sure the prayer-questions are smart ones. This should be daily practice with pen and paper.

Remember: the human nervous system, including the brain, always chooses pleasure over pain. Most of our lives revolve around these two parameters.

Ten Good Reasons

If I have things I should be doing but my being is resisting (eg giving up drugs; doing the tax return; exercising), I write down ten ways I will feel more pleasure if I do the thing. Then I write down ten ways I will feel more pain if I don't.

Writing ten things makes it clearer. I find that my brain, unconsciously, starts to select pleasure over pain, and I always effortlessly shift towards the thing I should be doing, over a period of a few hours or days. This process also works well for goals.

As you work with these ideas you'll discover how much power you actually have over the way you experience your life. Keep practising – it works. I wish you all the best.

Appendix 5 – Resources

There are so many resources for 12 Step groups! You'll find the ones I like best listed here. I've started with books because I love the feel of a book in my hand, particularly when I want to curl up and read.

Books

The books mentioned in the text of this book are available through the Powerfully Recovered Bookstore: http://www.powerfullyrecovered.com/book/listed.htm as well as other online and most brick and mortar bookstores. They are also listed here.

Alcoholics Anonymous
The *Big Book* - this is the true source of all 12 Step programs. A must for all 12 Steppers.
Paper. Often on back order. You can also find it at any AA group or office.

Twelve Steps & Twelve Traditions
This is the *12 & 12* - textbook to the 12 Steps and 12 Traditions - also a must if you're serious.
Hardcover – often on back order. You can also find it at any AA group or office.

As Bill Sees It
Selection of Bill W's writings, source of quotes
in *Powerfully Recovered!* Subject index.
Hardcover,often on back order. You can also find it at any
AA group or office.

A Reference Guide to the Big Book of Alcoholics Anonymous
by Stewert C.
An actual index or concordance to the *Big Book.* Great for
research or just checking things out.

The Varieties of Religious Experience
by William James
Deep, rich and important to the forming of 12 Step
spirituality - worth the effort.

Many Roads, One Journey - Moving Beyond the Twelve Steps
by Charlotte Davis Kasl
A truly awe inspiring book which contributes much to 12
Step thinking. Not light reading, but perfect for dipping into
and exploring. Kasel offers an alternative set of steps I find
too long and complicated, but the rest of the book is
wonderful. I strongly recommend this book!

How Alcoholics Anonymous Failed Me - My Personal Journey to Sobriety Through Self-Empowerment
by Marianne W. Gilliam
A throw the baby out with the bathwater book. Interesting if
you're doing research or want a way to avoid a 12 Step
Program, but disappointing for many of us.

The Handbook of Nonsexist Writing
by Casey Miller and Kate Swift

Out of print, but Amazon will get it for you in about two weeks - worth the wait!

Every week or so I review a book on my website. You'll find an index of the reviewed books at: http://www.powerfullyrecovered.com/book/reviewix.htm You can buy them online there or at many other online and brick and mortar bookstores. Some of my favorites are listed below.

Earth Prayers
There's a prayer a day here and each one puts you in touch with yourself and your relationship to our green and blue planet.

The book is designed to take you through the wheel of the year in seven sections, but the pages are undated, so you can start any time. If you're feeling disciplined, start at the front and work your way through. Or use it almost as an oracle by letting the book open where it will.

There is a special section called Benediction for the Animals. Another meditations portion provides an excellent starting point for getting quiet and listening to the 'still small voice.'
There is also a Calendar of Earth Prayers which groups many of the prayers by month.

No matter how you use it, this is a book that you will cherish and come back to again and again. It makes a truly wonderful gift as well.

The Tao of Womanhood -Ten Lessons for Power and Peace
Power and peace - who could ask for more? Diane Dreher has taken the Tao Te Ching, that two-thousand year old, multi-translated guide to living, and gently feminized it. Very gently, and very effectively.

After all, when Lao-tzu wrote it, he was addressing men as he searched for alternatives to war and conflict. Most translations have maintained that masculine tone. Dreher, recognizing the value in the distaff voice, honors the original.
She includes the Yin of Inner Peace, and the Yang of Personal Power. The way they are presented makes the contrast, and the similarities if not obvious, at least accessible.

With Lessons in Oneness, Centering and Natural Cycles, along with Lessons of timing, Courage, Strength and Agency, this is a book for our time without a doubt.
Another one to read straight through or dip in as you will, or both. Perfect gift for the women in your life, young and old.

The Courage to Be Rich: Creating a Life of Material and Spiritual Abundance
by Suze Orman
Not having enough money and not handling what you have well is a place of powerlessness. On the other hand, facing up to the truth about you and your money is a beginning of stepping into your power.

Suze Orman asks potent questions about your first ideas around money, paving the way to help you let go of damaging money myths.

A large part of this book encourages us to truly value ourselves and our money. Orman shows how financial abundance and spirituality can work hand-in-hand.

The book is also full of plain old practical advice. She doesn't assume you know about money, and she doesn't talk down to you either. Although some of the stories she uses seem like over simplification to me, most of the book is truly helpful and inspiring.

I particularly like her section on the Courage to Face the Unknown, which might have been titled 'what you need to get conscious about your money.'

She also has sections on home ownership, love and money, and planning for the future. There are exercises that will not only increase your awareness about you and your money, but will help you get organized as well.

This is not a book you'll read once. Rather, it is more like a reference book you'll refer to again and again over time.

Web Sites

There are literally thousands of web sites dealing with 12 Step Recovery and what might be called personal empowerment. Here are some of the best. Keep in mind, however, that the web changes faster than material printed on paper possibly can. For updates and additions, check: http://www.powerfullyrecovered.com/

Official 12 Step Sites

It seems as if there is a 12 Step group to handle almost any condition. New ones spring up all the time. These are the official websites of the organizations in question. The list is undoubtedly not complete – let me know what I've left out (wayman@inetworld.net) and I'll include it on my web site, and include it in the next edition of the book.

Alcoholics Anonymous - in English, French and Spanish:
http://www.alcoholics-anonymous.org

Al-Anon - which also includes information for teens:
http://www.al-anon.org

Adult Children of Alcoholics - with links to local meetings
http://www.adultchildren.org

Cocaine Anonymous - includes contacts, meetings. Also available in French.
http://www.ca.org/

Co-Dependents Anonymous - with meeting lists
http://www.codependents.org/index.html

Debtors Anonymous - including meeting information
http://www.debtorsanonymous.org/

Emotions Anonymous – for people who want to become
healthy emotionally.
http://emotionsanonymous.org/

Food Addicts Anonymous - aimed at helping those addicted
to food.
http://www.foodaddictsanonymous.org/newdefault.htm

Gamblers Anonymous - program and contact information
http://www.gamblersanonymous.org/

Marijuana Anonymous - FAQs, meeting information,
mailing lists. Some available in Spanish
http://www.marijuana-anonymous.org/

Nicotine Anonymous - meeting information, literature.
Available in German, French and Portuguese.
http://nicotine-anonymous.org/

Narcotics Anonymous - including meeting lists:
http://www.na.org/

Overeaters Anonymous - meeting, program and other
information.
http://www.OvereatersAnonymous.org/

Recovering Couples Anonymous - the focus here is couples
working the 12 Steps together.
http://www.recovering-couples.org/

Non-official, but helpful 12 Step sites

The sites listed here are my favorites, for any number of reasons. You'll find more on my web site:
http://www.powerfullyrecovered.com

12 Step Recovery at Bellaonline – I'm the host at this site. Articles, chat rooms a forum, products, etc.
http://www.bellaonline.com - in the health channel.

Alcoholism at About[37] - a solid resource with a newsletter, chat rooms, online meetings, a forum, etc.
http://alcoholsim@about.com

The Cult of Powerlessness - by an NA member in Australia, this salty essay is right on - so is the rest of the site, including the cartoons. Also a good collection of not so typical recovery links.
http://www.acay.com.au/~narcosis/Cult.htm

Alcoholism Index - this searchable index just gets better all the time. Good listing of Gay/Lesbian links too.
http://www.alcoholismhelp.com/

Alcohol and Drug Abuse - a solid overview of the problem and some surprisingly good links to books etc.
http://www.alcoholanddrugabuse.com/

Annie's Pages - Lots of solid and fun resources here including cards, an ezine and more - worth a look.
http://www.geocities.com/~acitygirl/

---

[37] I am an About guide. My site (http://sandiego.miningco.com) doesn't deal with 12 Step recovery although local 12 Step resources are listed there.

Alcoholism Treatment Info - Solid Q&A's about alcoholism and addictions with descriptions about different kinds of treatment. You can also reach an AA member directly through these pages.
http://www.alcoholismtreatment.org/

Anonymous One - a ton of links to meetings and other 12 Step resources. Also in Espanol!
http://www.anonymousone.com/main.htm

Bart's Page - creative, fun and helpful. Check out his Resentment Chart – sometimes slow enough to load to cause one, but worth it if you're hurting.
http://www.mindspring.com/~bartgr91/

The **Big Book**, chapter by chapter and with important areas singled out. Although there isn't a search engine here, if your browser allows it, a keyword search could be done.
http://www.recovery.org/aa/bigbook/ww/

CyberSober - offers over 150,000 anonymous meetings with maps. BUT a fee is required.
http://cybersober.com/

Find a Meeting - an extensive list of face-to-face meetings organized by state.
http://soberspace.com/

Gay/Lesbian Recovery - meeting lists around the country, some articles.
 http://www.atlantaguy.com/recovery.htm

Grant Me Serenity - a beautiful site with all sorts of helpful information. Powerfully Recovered is listed there.
http://Open-Mind.org/

H.O.W. Recovery - Honest, Open, Willing - good 12 Step links here.
http://www.whitemtns.com/~tsa/recovery/

Jaywalker - excellent resources, including a downloadable Fourth Step Guide (+ an inventory for groups) as well as his own Big Book Twelve Step Guides and a truly cool treatment of the Big Book's "Doctors Opinion" Plus the Carl Jung/Bill W letter - a must!
http://TheJaywalker.Com

Jews In Recovery - there's a ton of good information here for anyone.
http://www.jacsweb.org/

Lifescape - good self-help and other mental health resources. Online experts often available in real time. Good addiction resources as well.
http://www.lifescape.com/

Online Recovery - a good index of AA and NA and most other 12 Step sites.
http://www.onlinerecovery.org/index.html

Recoveries Anonymous - the emphasis here is on the positive side of recovery - great idea, some free stuff, some they charge for.
http://www.r-a.org/

Recovery Connection - has a paid membership as well as lots of free stuff. Worth a look.
http://www.recoveryconnection.com/

Recovery Reality - real recovery humor. He's got a book, a column and if you're lucky, you'll catch a performance.
http://www.marklundholm.com/

Recovered Alcoholics - Yep, sounds like our kind of place. They've got their own bookstore and their own book. Check it out.
http://www.recoveredalcoholics.com/

Recovered Alcoholics Bookstore - No, I didn't start this one, but I might have. And Powerfully Recovered! is there, right along with some other great titles.
http://www.recoveredalcoholics.com/bookstore.htm

Sober Times - honors the 12 Steps and respects non-traditional approaches.
http://www.sobertimes.com/

Spiritual History and Roots of Early A.A. - Great reading for any 12 Stepper. Dick B. has also written some interesting books about the history of A.A.
http://www.dickb.com/index.shtml

Sober 24 - Daily readings, chat, shopping etc
http://www.sober24.com/

Something Fishy - from a reader, all about eating disorders.
http://www.something-fishy.org/

Empowering Sites

These are sites I feel really help us become and stay Powerfully Recovered! Some are 12 Step sites; many are not.

Spiritual sites

Spiritual can be an iffy definition – while my criteria is flexible, one of my major requirements is a lack of dogma. I want open-mindedness and a willingness to question, coupled with the ability to accept new and other ideas.

12 Steps and the Course in Miracles - uses the powerful Course in Miracles to support a 12 Step spiritual awakening. http://12stepprograms.hypermart.net/

16 Steps - ok, that's maybe a few too many, but it's based on the wonderful *Many Roads, One Journey* book and worth a look for sure. From the same source is more information. http://members.tripod.com/~NadineGaye/16steps.htm

Beliefnet – a major portal site with teachings and links from all sorts of spiritual disciplines. http://www.beliefnet.com

Believe - you may want to bookmark this one when you need a spiritual break. http://www.ishaah.com/Believe.htm

Bellaonline – there's a Pagan site here and a Tarot site – look under Society and Culture.
http://www.bellaonline.com

Fifth Goddess - a lovely site worth exploring - empower yourself!
http://www.fifthgoddess.com/

InnerVoice - A solid and growing collection of self-help, recovery, spirituality and just good living.
http://www.geocities.com/~enchantedlakes/innervoice/

Intervention Organization - fascinating! Art as healing - sometimes shocking, always worth a look.
http://members.nbci.com/socialwork/

Pagan/Wiccan at About – a rich resource.
http://paganwiccan.about.com/

Spirit Haven - web home of Ruth Fishel, who wrote *Precious Solitude*, offers affirmations, women's workshops in Cape Cod (tempting), a newsletter and more.
http://www.spirithaven.com/

Pagan Links

I've found pagan or earth-based spirituality to be particularly satisfying.

Covenant of Unitarian Universalist Pagans, Inc. (CUUPS) – the earth based arm of UU.
http://www.cuups.org/content/intro.html

Goddess Breath in Stone - A beautiful book, in all senses of the word. Part of Freedom Editions.

http://www.inficad.com/~freedomeditions/goddess/goddess.
htm

The **Pagan Recovery Project** - provides a printable version
of their 12 Steps and a simple ritual.
http://www.wenet.net/user/rhys/12steps.htm

Self-Help

Self-help is another term that can be interpreted in any
number of ways. On the net, there are many so-called sites
that are thinly disguised sales pitches. Others make a real
effort to offer something in addition to their products. Each
of the sites here has a great deal to offer.

Self-Help Psychology Magazine - has an amazing
collection of helpful pages.
http://www.shpm.com/

Self Improvement Online - is doing a good job of gathering
all sorts of self-help together in one spot. Check out my
article there. Or take an IQ or other quiz for fun.
http://www.selfgrowth.com/index.html

Origami - ok, this site is about the art of folding paper into
wonderful shapes and mental health, but there are directions
for making all sorts of wonderful things.
http://free.prohosting.com/~origami/

The Rules of Being Human - a single page that's worth
reading every now and again.
http://sendafriend.com/beinghuman/

Business/Career

Although I've been known to balk at the term 'earn a living,' I
do know that how we work is tremendously important. If I

could wave a magic wand, everyone would be able to do exactly the type of work they truly wanted to do.

These links, and many of them are aimed at writers, offer solid help in the practical side of pursuing dreams.

Booklocker - If you've got an ebook, these people do a great job. And Angela knows marketing inside and out. I have an ebook there. It's called *How To Write A Non-Fiction Book Proposal That Sells* and you'll find it at: http://www.booklocker.com/bookpages/annewayman01.html The whole site is worth looking at, even if you don't want to write. There's fiction and non-fiction. http://www.booklocker.com

Business and You - probably the most powerful business seminar on the planet - perfect for organizations that must have team building. http://www.businessandu.com

Empowerment Resources - I've just gotten started exploring this site, which focuses on personal, social and ecological empowerment. There are so many links, articles and other information it's a bit overwhelming. http://www.empowermentresources.com/index.html

Empowermenttech - I'm the webmaster here; I've worked with Bill Wright on a number of projects and can attest to the fact he's a great coach for a group or an individual. http://www.empowermenttech.com

GetLifeLinedUp - I've done some teleclasses here and they are great! I enjoy the newsletter too. http://www.GetLifeLinedUp.com

Life On Purpose - coaching of all sorts, free resources. http://www.lifeonpurpose.com/

Molly Gordon - is a personal and business coach with teleclasses and outstanding resources on her pages - including a vision quest for your business. Knows artists and how to help them move comfortable in the business arena. http://www.mollygordon.com/coach.html

Motivator Pro - Goal Setting redefined - I've fallen in love with this software - it allows me to set and see the big picture, add spiritual quotes and questions, and generally keep me on track. Their site has some great philosophy and you can download a 30-day trial for free. Truly powerful. http://www.motivator.com/entrance.cfm?Dealer_ID=10440

Seminar Finder - if you're looking for a seminar you may find it here - fun to browse. http://www.seminarmaster.com/

Super Wisdom - resources and reasonably priced courses for sales people and entrepreneurs drawing from Vernon Howard's teaching. He's known for clear distillations of ancient wisdom. http://www.superwisdom.com/

Tips Products International – Paulette Ensign bills herself as Chief Visionary and I it's true. She offers some of the most practical marketing information and how-to I've ever found, and much of it requires sweat equity rather than cash. http://tipsbooklets.com/

Upublish - the publisher of my book - print on demand and ebook versions. Excellent! http://www.upublish.com

If these don't provide the information you're looking for, try your favorite search engine and narrow your search

by being specific. My favorites are the meta-search engines –
that search engines. I use:

- http://mamma.com
- http://dogpile.com

Online Meetings

The Internet and the Web have opened up a whole new type of Fellowship – the online meeting. These are conducted in real-time through chat software. Conversations are conducted by typing which appears almost instantly on all participants' screens.

While it's certainly possible to share and learn in this manner, and although some of these sessions are truly valuable, there are some cautions.

First of all, you truly have no idea who is participating. You can't see them and you can't hear their voice, which means you're missing valuable clues. You can't, for instance, tell for sure if the person you're chatting with is male or female, old or young. Nor is there any way to sense how long they've really been working the Program except in what they say.

Online meetings are places to be particularly careful about checking things out for yourself.

The other major issue is protecting your own anonymity, and not just to avoid having people know your participating in 12 Step recovery. You need to be extra careful online to make sure you're not setting yourself up for abuse.

For instance, most chat programs will allow you to enter your email address or not. My suggestion is don't do it. If, over time, you find you want to connect with another chat member, you can reveal your email to them privately – if the software doesn't allow this, change to a chat room that does.

That said, I've found online meetings to be a great resource. One of the most interesting and important things about them is that you can almost always find one. I've had the best luck with the scheduled meetings at: http://alcoholism.about.com/mpchat.htm.

Buddy T., the Guide there, currently has four chat rooms. Two are open 24 hours a day and you can drop in anytime. The other two are actually scheduled meetings, and you'll find a schedule posted at the above link. The emphasis is on AA, Al-Anon, and ACOA, but I wouldn't be surprised to find other groups springing up there over time.

If you hang out online, you'll eventually find one or two people you may want to meet face-to-face. Again, proceed with caution.

Start with private email and if that goes well, go to phone calls with no addresses. If you still want to meet them, do so in a public place and make sure you have your own transportation.

I have two close friends I've met online, but I've also stopped communicating with people who started to sound weird, and I've never put myself in a position where they can find me. You would do well to do the same.

Telephone Numbers

Finding the phone number to a particular 12 Step office or meeting is often a matter of checking the white pages in the phone book or asking information to find it for you. This is particularly true in major metropolitan areas in the U.S. I have had some luck locating less well known 12 Step groups by calling the local Alcoholics Anonymous office.

Here are the national offices of some of the major 12 Step organizations:

- Alcoholics Anonymous World Services - (212) 870-3400
- New York, NY
- Al-Anon (toll free) – 1-888-4AL-ANON - Virginia Beach, VA
- Adult Children of Alcoholics – (310) 534-1815 Torrance, CA)
- Cocaine Anonymous - (310) 559-5833 – Los Angeles, CA
- Co-Dependents Anonymous – (602) 277-7991 – Phoenix, AZ
- Debtors Anonymous – (781) 453-2743 - Needam, MA
- Food Addicts Anonymous – (561) 967-3871 – West Palm Beach, FL
- Gamblers Anonymous - (213) 386-8789 – Los Angeles, CA
- Marijuana Anonymous – (toll free) 800 766-6779 – Van Nuys, CA

- Narcotics Anonymous – (818) 773-9999 - Los Angeles CA
- Overeaters Anonymous (505) 891-2664 – Rio Rancho NM
- Recovering Couples Anonymous - (636) 397-0867 - Chesterfield, MO

Finding Contacts When You're Not In The United States

Alcoholics Anonymous meetings can probably be found in every country, and in every language, in the world. They are easiest to find in English speaking western countries. French and Spanish speakers will find AA meetings in the appropriate countries fairly easily.

If you're planning ahead, you can find AA International General Service offices at:

http://aa.org/english/IntGSO/E_IntGSO_d1.html

Some 35 countries are listed there, and the site is updated frequently.

The Alcoholism Index provides another, fairly extensive listing of meetings in countries around the world at:

http://www.alcoholismhelp.com/index/html/sgp112.html

It gets more interesting if you're wandering the world, but it's not impossible. If a telephone directory is available, start there – assuming the country uses a western style alphabet you may be surprised and find a listing.

If you're staying at a hotel, or even a hostel, ask – again, you may be pleasantly surprised to find someone there knows what you're talking about. You can also make good use of bulletin boards – post a notice either asking for AA or, if you want to protect your anonymity, ask for friends of Bill W.

Police departments are another source of possible information, so are embassies and churches. You may have to do some serious poking around. In some countries, the meetings may be seriously secret, so be patient.

You may find yourself in a meeting and you don't understand the language. Go for it! The sense of the meeting will be the same, and someone will have a few words of English.

If all else fails, start your own meeting. I did this in the Kingdom of Tonga on the island of Vava'u. I started by going to the local Catholic Church. There was an Irish priest there and he not only spoke English, he knew about AA and had a *Big Book* that someone had left the year before. We agreed on a meeting room, day and time. He spread the word and so did I. Our first meeting, four people showed up; the second four again, but not the same four. In the second group was an Englishman who was spending the year on the island. He agreed to take over and continue the meeting. I have no idea if it lasted – but it worked for me and for several others while we were there.

Other 12 Step groups can be harder to find. Narcotics Anonymous is probably the second most likely, particularly in western countries. Don't be shy. If you're a member of OA, GA or some other 12 Step group and need a meeting, go to any 12 Step meeting you can find. You'll find you're welcome, no matter what your addiction/dysfunction is, as long as you are polite and respectful.

Appendix 6 - The 12 Steps of Alcoholics Anonymous[38]

1.   We admitted we were powerless over alcohol–that our lives had become unmanageable.

2.   Came to believe that a Power greater than ourselves could restore us to sanity.

3.   Made a decision to turn our will and our lives over to the care of God *as we understood God.*[39]

4.   Made a searching and fearless moral inventory of ourselves.

5.   Admitted to God, to ourselves, and to another human being the exact nature of our wrongs.

6.   Were entirely ready to have God remove all these defects of character.

---

[38] I've used the 12 Steps and 12 Traditions from Alcoholics Anonymous because they are the originals. It's interesting to note that there are only two references to alcohol in the Steps – in Step 1 and in Step 2. Twelve Step recovery groups simply substitute the name of the condition they are addressing.

[39] As explained in the Author's Notes at the beginning of this book, I have substituted the word 'God' for the gender-specific 'Him.'

7.   Humbly asked God to remove our shortcomings.

8.   Made a list of all persons we had harmed, and became willing to make amends to them all.

9.   Made direct amends to such people wherever possible, except when to do so would injure them or others.

10. Continued to take personal inventory and when we were wrong promptly admitted it.

11. Sought through prayer and meditation to improve our conscious contact with God *as we understood God*, praying only for the knowledge of God's will for us and the power to carry that out.

12. Having had a spiritual awakening as the result of these steps, we tried to carry this message to alcoholics, and to practice these principles in all our affairs

The 12 Traditions of Alcoholics Anonymous

1.   Our common welfare should come first; personal recovery depends upon A.A. unity.

2.   For our group purpose there is but one ultimate authority–a loving God as God may be expressed in our group conscience.

3.   The only requirement for A.A. membership is a desire to stop drinking.

4.   Each group should be autonomous except in matters affecting other groups or A.A. as a whole.

5.   Each group has but one primary purpose–to carry its message to the alcoholic who still suffers.

6.   An A.A. group ought never endorse, finance or lend the A.A. name to any related facility our outside enterprise, lest problems of money, property and prestige divert us from our primary purpose.

7.   Every A.A. group ought to be fully self-supporting, declining outside contributions.

8.   Alcoholics Anonymous should remain forever nonprofessional, but our service centers may employ special workers.

9.   A.A., as such, ought never be organized; but we may create service boards or committees directly responsible to those they serve.

10. Alcoholics Anonymous has no opinion on outside issues; hence the A.A. name ought never be drawn into public controversy.

11. Our public relations policy is based on attraction rather than promotion; we need always maintain personal anonymity at the level of press, radio and films.

12. Anonymity is the spiritual foundation of all our Traditions, ever reminding us to place principles before personalities.

My Web Sites

Currently, I have four websites (did you ever know an alcoholic to do things half-way?) That may be too many.

One is for this book:

http://www.powerfullyrecovered.com

It has, among other things, an online bookstore, book reviews, articles and additional links dealing with recovery and personal growth.

Another site is:

http://www.whengrandmotherspeaks.com

It draws its name from the (I suspect) American Indian saying:

When Grandmother speaks the planet will
be healed.

The first time I heard this I got chills all through my body!

Here you will find an eclectic selection, which reflect my growing concerns and grief about our planet and our way of life and other things – it's my place to sound off to the world.

I'm also a host for Bellaonline, a portal for women. My topic is 12 Step Recovery which you can find by going to the Health Channel at

http://bellaonline.com

I'm also About's Guide to San Diego:

http://sandiego.about.com

Ecards

When I need a break, I sometimes put together free ecards. Some of them are digital photos that I've taken, others are artwork I've bought or otherwise acquired along the way.

You can find them at:

http://www.powerfullyrecovered.com/resources/cards.htm

Acknowledgements

I've had amazing help with this edition of Powerfully Recovered! Narcosis not only contributed the cartoons, but did some loving and telling copy editing as a well. Douglas. W. keeps giving the book positive reviews every time he gets the chance. Kathe Neilson, Donna and Ellie Winslow also keep offering support and needed handholding.

My friend, Narcosis, not only contributed both the cartoons and the essay on emotions, but did a stellar job of proofreading as well. The errors are mine, however.

Kara and Ian did an outstanding job on the cover.

I'm so pleased with Uplublish.com – the official publisher of Powerfully Recovered! When I launched the first edition as a Print On Demand I didn't realize what a great service they offered.

In fact, as you might be able to tell, I am truly blessed and grateful.

Index

Powerfully Recovered!

Text designed by

Anne Wayman
Composed aboard my boat on San Diego Bay
On a PC using Word and Adobe

Cover designed by:

Kera McHugh and Ian Backs
somethingelse web+graphics
http://www.time4somethingelse.com

Cartoons by:

Narcosis
http://fly.to/dragoncomix.

Powerfully Recovered website:

http://powerfullyrecovered.com

Order Powerfully Recovered!

The publishing revolution created by Print On Demand and Ebooks means you have many choices. Bookstores may have the paperback version, and if they don't, they are able to order it easily.

Online you can purchase the paperback version from the following websites:

Powerfully Recovered!
http://www.powerfullyrecovered.com
Upublish
http://www.upublish.com/books/wayman.htm
Amazon
http://www.amazon.com/exec/obidos/ASIN/1581128762/o/q
id=973961236/sr=8-1/powerfurecoverac
Borders
http://borders.com
Barnes and Noble
http://bn.com

The ebook version is available at:

Powerfully Recovered!
http://www.powerfullyrecovered.com
Upublish
http://www.upublish.com/books/wayman.htm

Lifekits
John Nicolson is developing an ebook version of Powerfully Recovered! in one of his Lifekits, along with other items concerning addiction and recovery.
Lifekits is at: http://www.lifekits.com
The kit, "Power Over Alcohol", which includes Powerfully Recovered! will be available soon in the Health/Addiction Therapy category at Lifekits.

For review copies, quantity discounts and other special requests email the author at:

wayman@inetworld.net

or send your request to:

Anne Wayman
1880 Harbor Is. Dr.
San Diego, CA 92101
USA

CPSIA information can be obtained at www.ICGtesting.com
Printed in the USA
BVOW08s1640040915

416542BV00001B/40/P